Royal Albert Hall in London, England
1970

THE GUITAR
BEHIND DYLAN & COHEN
© 2017 by Ron Cornelius

Published by Gateway Entertainment Inc.
Music publishing and production since 1994.
www.GatewayEntertainment.com

Original cover artwork and all original interior drawings
by Vladislav Filipovic.

Special thanks to book creator, Brian Mast, and his publishing
company (www.BookRipple.com) for his help with this project.

ISBN: 978-1-943157-29-7

Library of Congress Control Number: 2016948346

Printed in the United States of America

HOW TO ORDER:

www.GatewayEntertainment.com

Tin Luck Series: Vol. 1

RON CORNELIUS

THE

GUITAR

BEHIND DYLAN & COHEN

THE GUITAR

1959 Grestch
"Country Gentleman"
For Ron Cornelius, by Grestch

The "Country Gentleman" by Grestch was introduced in 1959, the only year that the "Country Gentleman" was hand-made. From 1960 on it has been a production-line instrument.

As a promotional campaign, the company presented several "Country Gentleman" guitars at a tremendous discount to accomplished young players. In my area, one went to southern California and one to northern California. I was selected to receive the one for northern California. I met the man who assembled the guitar, and during this "prototype year," I was able to choose from four different necks. I could not wait until the guitar arrived!

Most players over the course of a career own many different instruments. Session players, as a rule, have a wall full of guitars, which they use to earn a living. My case was different for I played this one guitar throughout a forty-year career. From dusty bars and nightclubs to the most prestigious concert halls in the world, from Sam's Club to Royal Albert Hall and Vienna Opera House, it was this one guitar.

For over forty years this guitar has been in the fast lane, possibly more than any guitar on the planet, in concert, touring, or recording albums with the biggest of the big.

This guitar has been written up as "The Guitar Behind Dylan & Cohen" and its discography list includes Bob Dylan, Leonard Cohen, Johnny Cash, Flatt & Scruggs, Louden Wainright III, Willie Nelson, and many, many more. I believe this list to be unmatchable for any one guitar.

As a point of interest, notice the famous VOX Python strap on the guitar. It's been on the guitar for over forty years. The reason being: at the beginning of the "British Invasion," spearheaded by the Beatles, Vox entered the U.S. market by hiring a San Francisco based marketing firm by the name of Cambell Ewald Agency. As part of their promotional campaign, they produced a full album demonstrating the entire Vox line of instruments and accessories. My band was hired as the musicians to make this album. The public, or Vox for that matter, never knew that every guitar sound and every guitar accessory demoed was recorded with my Grestch "Country Gentleman."

As payment, apart from our Union Recording Scale, we were given "Super Beatle" amps, guitars, drums, keyboards and tons of accessories made by Vox. The amps were great but the instruments were not and the only thing that survived the test of time is the Python strap. It is still there today.

This Custom Handmade 1959 Gretsch "Country Gentleman," in the hands of Ron Cornelius, has been in concert, on tour, or on the albums of:

Bob Dylan	Leonard Cohen
Johnny Cash	Charlie Daniels
Willie Nelson	Tracy Nelson

Glen Campbell Aretha Franklin
The Lettermen Chubby Checker
Smokey Robinson and the Miracles
Chris Gray Miko Marks
Jernie Dinah and the Desert Crusaders
Michael Grimm Billy Joe Shaver
The Kingston Trio Sonny and Cher
Annette Funicello Loudon Wainwright III
Mickey Carroll Lester Flatt
Earl Scruggs Flatt and Scruggs
Hoyt Axton The Righteous Brothers
Buddy Hyatt Paula McCulla
David Allen Coe Aldo Calabrese
Bobby Freeman The Shirelles
Gladys Knight and the Pips
The Chiffons Gene Chandler
Gene Pitney Johnny Morrisette
H.B. Barnum Jan and Dean
Sly Stewart Mary Wells
The Coasters Clairette Clementino
The Diamonds Paul and Paula
Freddie Hart Harland Sanders
Ella Fitzgerald Bertha Tillman
Little Anthony and the Imperials
Wally Cox Connie Francis
Jimmy Clanton Billy Storm
Dick and Dee Dee Carol Connors
Robert Conrad Marty Balin
Johnny Crawford Dinah Washington
Connie Stevens Little "E"
Kathy Young Jimmy Flint and the Stones
The Individuals Gram Bell
Carol Grimes Tracy Nelson
Mirabai Jackie Wilson
Martha and the Vandellas

The Whites   Paul Hampton
Freddy Cannon   The Untouchables
Ron Cornelius   West

I Walk The Line (Motion Picture Soundtrack)
Concrete Cowboy (Motion Picture Soundtrack)
The Big Labouski (Motion Picture Sountrack)
Little Fauss and Big Halsy (Motion Picture Soundtrack)

and many more!

WHAT OTHERS ARE SAYING

Ron Cornelius, Guitar Wizard who Toured and Recorded With Bob Dylan, Leonard Cohen. and Johnny Cash, Tells What It Was Really Like in Must-Read Book, *The Guitar Behind Dylan & Cohen*

The
New York
Times

—By PHIL SWEETLAND
Music & radio contributor

NASHVILLE — Bob Dylan and Leonard Cohen are two of the most important but enigmatic singers and songwriters in pop history, and both were brilliant enough to hire many of the greatest sidemen of their times.

One session player Cohen and Dylan both treasured and still work with is the guitar maestro Ron Cornelius, who played on seven multi-platinum Dylan albums including *Self Portrait* and *New Morning* and four more from Cohen, notably *Songs Of Love And Hate* and *Songs From A Room*, all the while working as bandleader for seven of Leonard's world tours in the late Sixties and early Seventies.

Now Ron has collected many of his fondest memories, road adventures, and first-person Cohen and Dylan insights in a book called *The Guitar Behind Dylan & Cohen* that will be treasured by fans of all ages who have loved and studied the music and lives of these great artists for nearly 50 years.

In her foreword to the book, the British journalist and Cohen biographer Sylvie Simmons recalls the day she received the draft of Ron's book and started reading his recollections. "I was rapt," Simmons writes, "that's the kind of stories."

So many of the rock and pop heroes of the Sixties and Seventies are either now dead or were so wasted in those days that they remember nearly nothing. Cornelius, however, had a love for nothing stronger than cognac and fine cigars, and his recollections remain sharp as a tack.

"You never knew what Leonard Cohen might do or say that could cause things to get very weird," Ron writes. One time, Leonard performed an entire encore while standing on his head, and at another show he caused a near riot at a show in Hamburg by suddenly doing a Nazi salute.

Another fascinating insight Cornelius gives us is this: "It was always strange to me that whenever we toured outside the United States, Leonard was number one in the people's eyes, and Dylan was number two. However, once back in the USA, Dylan was always number one and no one even seemed to know who Leonard was," Ron writes.

Nashville in the late 1960s and early 1970s could be a tough place for longhaired California musicians like Cornelius, but when he came here to record with Dylan, the equally eccentric Dylan producer Bob Johnston, and session superstars including Charlie Daniels and Kenny Buttrey, Ron knew they were making music history.

"Dylan's song-by-song approach was nothing like I'd been around and took getting used to," Cornelius recalls. Dylan would vary tempos markedly between takes, a real challenge for the musicians, but Ron notes that "the waterfall of material coming from Dylan was constant and overwhelming."

Bob loved Ron's guitar solo on "New Morning," recorded at CBS Studios in New York, and asked Cornelius if there was anything he could get Ron to return the favor. After everyone else had left, Cornelius asked Dylan to sit down at the piano with a guitar on his lap and play Ron's favorite Dylan songs as he lay on the floor. For the next half hour, Cornelius lay down next to the piano as Dylan gave him a one-on-one concert of Ron's favorite Bob Dylan compositions.

There are tales of the European tours with Cohen, when they played not only at legendary concert halls but at insane asylums, many of which were more like prisons. There were road pranks all over the world played by Johnston, Charlie Daniels, and Cornelius, sometimes involving airport security and other times involving loaded guns pointed at the boys in the band.

Cornelius also recollects the writing process he contributed to several famous songs, including Cohen's "Chelsea Hotel #2," a story song about Leonard, an unmade bed, and Janis Joplin: and "Jerusalem," which Ron wrote while he was touring the Holy City and later became a breakout hit for the Israeli superstar Esther Ofarim.

Finally, Ron takes us inside San Quentin Prison with Johnny Cash for Johnny's legendary live recording there in the winter of 1969. Of all the musicians and producers on hand, Cornelius was likely the only one who had ever been to

Quentin before, visiting convict friends of his from his tough teen years in the Bay Area town of Richmond.

Do yourself a favor. Get out those Dylan and Cohen albums, pick up a copy (or several copies) of Ron Cornelius's *The Guitar Behind Dylan & Cohen*, and read as you listen to learn what you never knew about the records and the artists you thought you knew so well.

WHAT OTHERS ARE SAYING

A Music Industry Leader's Life on the Road and in the Studio With Some of the World's Greatest in *The Guitar Behind Dylan & Cohen*

—By Joanne Marlowe
Owner/CEO UFT/Chicago

What an indulgence! To hear first-hand accounts drawn from a life glowing with such musical color and celebrity personalities that the reader is able to slip vicariously into a private "on request" concert by Bob Dylan or experience the deeply touching sentiments expressed by a crowd of appreciative Israelis in a Jerusalem concert hall or the exhilaration of barreling down a snow-covered highway with Charlie Daniels giving a jovial performance from his position sprawled across the back seat. These are the type of one-of-a-kind pleasures derived from the down-home anthology of autobiographical creative non-fiction essays composed and compiled by Ron Cornelius.

Ron has been on the road with music legends dating back to Jan and Dean, traveled the world over recording with an array of celebrity artists including Leonard Cohen and Bob Dylan, and been a part of country music history on several occasions including contributing to the production of the *Live From San*

Quentin album which was cut by Johnny Cash within the walls of the penitentiary of that name. For those of us who have never known the pleasure of standing center stage in Radio City Music Hall or basked in the grandeur of The Royal Albert Hall in London, a stroll through Ron's memory banks is a once in a lifetime opportunity to bring a common man into the truly uncommon and often times serial world of celebrity music.

Stylistically, this collection of individual essays is an easy read which resonates with the friendly and open charm of an old-world storyteller that gleefully invites the listener to step into his world for a fleeting moment.

In short, this collection proves that the art of storytelling has not been lost. Ron skillfully spins a yarn which molds the readers' consciousness into a miniature replica of his own, taking care to measure his remarks with near surgical precision to assure that his enthusiasm for the subject matter doesn't spoil the oftentimes ironic humor which underlies his stories like a well-crafted punch-line to an elaborate joke.

Unexpectedly, but quite logically, the tales told within the pages of this collection provide a rare glimpse into the human condition from a totally unique perspective—one of the fish looking out from the fishbowl. Music, especially music as deeply touching as that of Dylan and Cohen, evokes a response from its audiences which is replete with the genuine-ness of true heartfelt emotion and, if truly captured in a moment of artistic bliss, one that transcends explanation except by poetic metaphor or a precise retelling of the events leading up to that moment.

Ron, again and again, captures those rare moments with an ease of conversational writing style that makes such a feat appear effortless. He adeptly shares with the reader those spontaneous events when, through the appreciation of the art by the audience and the baring of the idiosyncrasies of the performers, inclusive of his own, both the simplicity and complexity of the human condition becomes paradoxically and enchantingly evident.

Ron has had the pleasure of observing people at their most genuine moments in life. To the performer, that is the instant when inspiration and divinity manifest in the music. To the audience, that is the instant when the audience truly becomes part of the communal art and the spirit is touched by that gentle impact of melody and lyric. This collection weaves together the threads of a life well-sampled into a tapestry of many colors which is sure to bring a smile to the face of the reader while taking in the sights and sounds of Ron's days on the road and in the studio, but is sure to leave behind meaningful jewels of anecdotal lessons learned which will be treasured by the reader for times to come.

This book takes on a life of its own with a simplicity that conveys the beauty, pleasure, charm and humor of a truly uncommon collection of experiences in a way that is sure to connect with the "everyman" while offering tasteful insights into the lives and personalities of some of the world's most famous performers which will engross even a passive music enthusiast. There is no doubt that the reader is set for a feast which promises exotic flavors of uncommon origins when they join Ron on a short walk down memory lane in these fast-paced essays.

DEDICATION

My first trip to Nashville, Tennessee was in the mid-60s.

In Nashville, I was warned, you could kick trees and great guitar players would fall down out of them.

I was even told that when you get to Nashville, pull over at the outskirts of town and buy gasoline—and if you can outplay the guy pumping your gas, go on into town—if not, turn around and go home.

You can imagine how I felt 50 years later standing in front of the Ron Cornelius exhibit in the, one and only, Country Music Hall of Fame.

I dedicate this book to every young musician out there who is NOT WILLING *to turn around and go home!*

—Ron Cornelius

FOREWORD

Ron Cornelius has stories.

I heard a bunch of them the first time we talked (for my big, fat book on Leonard Cohen) and whenever our paths have crossed since then from a brewery in Northern California where Ron once had a band called "West," to a stage in Nashville, where he moved four decades back and stayed on to become a lauded Music City fixture—I've heard even more. One day the mailman arrived with a package full of stories he'd written about when he was on the road. I was rapt. That's the kind of stories.

It doesn't hurt that he's spent a lifetime in music—much of that in a time when nothing, short of love, had the kind of power that music had in our lives. Ron had his first record deal when he was 16. In the early sixties, when rock-n-roll was king, he played with the likes of Chubby Checker, Little Anthony and Smokey Robinson. In the mid-to-late sixties, when folk-rock and country-rock ruled, Ron, who also played on albums with bluegrass stars Flatt & Scruggs, had his own hippie country-folk band, West.

The end of that remarkable decade and the beginning of the next found him working alongside some of the greatest musical icons of our time: Bob Dylan, Leonard Cohen, Johnny Cash.

When the Man in Black played his legendary San Quentin Prison concert, Ron was there with him, behind the bars. He was also there for Leonard Cohen's lesser-known mental asylum concerts (ask him to tell you the story about Leonard Cohen, Dennis Hopper and the audience at a state hospital in California wine country some time).

Ron, who's still close with Leonard, played a key role on two of his greatest early albums, *Songs From A Room* and *Songs Of Love and Hate*. He also co-wrote one of Cohen's best-loved songs, *Chelsea Hotel #2*—you know, the one about Leonard, Janis Joplin and an unmade bed.

Ron went around the world six times with Leonard Cohen. He was there, leading the band, for the heady, crazy tours of 1970 and 1972, when things got so out-there that the tour manager (Bill Donovan) made them hold hands walking through airports, so that he wouldn't lose anyone.

Oh, and ask him about the infamous 1970 Isle of Wight festival, when they had to go on after someone set the stage on fire during Jimi Hendrix's set. Or the time when a copious intake of wine and other substances led to their dicey ride up the ramp and onto the stage on horses. Or the gun-toting German fan, Brigitte Bardot. Or … well you've got the idea: Ron Cornelius has stories.

Here's Some To Be Getting On With.

—Sylvie Simmons

CONTENTS

INTRODUCTION

For many years, over, and over, people have told me that I should write a book about my life experiences in the music industry. Never gave that much thought until, at a point in time, the concept of individual "short-stories" came to mind. To write a book that's not a "tell-all" but one of true experiences that could appeal to music lovers and fans the world over. A book for people interested in knowing what it would be like to run in the fast lane as a guitar player.

To record with Bob Dylan, Leonard Cohen, Johnny Cash, Lester Flatt and Earl Scruggs, Charlie Daniels, Willie Nelson, Hoyt Axton, Louden Wainwright and on and on. To take the stage of sold out venues like The Royal Albert Hall in London, The Vienna Opera House, The Olympia Theater in Paris, or Tivoli Gardens in Copenhagen. To be part of a headline act at big concerts with thousands in attendance—and even the ultimate challenges like The Isle Of White with over 600,000 people in the audience.

But more over, and especially in my case, it's the life events that have gone on around all of this that can be unbelievable—unbelievable, but absolutely true.

The title of this book, "The Guitar Behind Dylan and Cohen," was the title of a two-page newspaper article that was written about me. I chose to use it because the stories (in this book) take place during the portion of my career at which time I was simultaneously recording albums with Bob Dylan and recording albums and touring with Leonard Cohen.

Most of the people in this book are known to be, and recognized as, great songwriters as well as being artists. However, Cohen and Dylan, and their use of music as a way to speak to the masses are a very different world. Being part of all that led me in and out of some of the dambdest situations imaginable.

As I share these stories with you, and as you read, put yourself in my shoes and let yourself become … the *guitar* behind Dylan and Cohen.

28

CHAPTER ONE

THE SMALL WORLD OF A GUITAR

Somewhere around the age of 10 or 11 I became interested in the idea of playing the guitar. I had played the Clarinet in grade school, switching to the Trombone in junior high, but neither of these instruments did much more for me other than providing something in my day that was enjoyable.

I liked singing in choir and glee clubs and, of course, you can't sing while playing trombone or—least I couldn't. They didn't offer lessons on the guitar in school, so if I did decide to get into this, it would be on my own time.

I then spent a period of time wanting a guitar and not having one. I remember regularly taking up my mother's broom, cutting a pick out of the sides of milk cartons and while holding the broom as though it were a guitar, working out rhythm patterns with my right hand.

When I finally got my first guitar for Christmas, I already had many strumming patterns mastered, thanks to that old broom. My only aspiration to begin with was to learn enough to be able to sit around a camp fire or party and play well enough to accompany myself, or someone else, who might want to sing a song.

Soon I accomplished that goal only to find it wasn't enough. So, I began taking guitar lessons and it wasn't long until I became obsessed. Spending four to six hours playing per day was not unusual. Being part of a band and playing at a dance or show was now my new goal.

Next, being able to hear some kind of recording of my playing became important. That desire was fulfilled in a tiny, garage-style, studio in my hometown—I still have that recording. I must have been 12 or 13 at the time. At age 14, I took delivery on a wonderful Guitar that would become the wooden ship I would ride all over the world.

A sort of research was done by the company that built this Guitar (Gretsch) and two students from our state, one in Northern California and one in Southern California, qualified to receive one at a reduced price.

The Guitar was the first of a line known as "The Country Gentleman." It was handmade for only one year because Gibson bought the company in 1960 and started mass machine production. I was able to meet the man who actually made this Guitar and chose from four different necks the one which suited me best.

In 1960 and 1961, this Guitar found itself on tour with Smoky Robinson & The Miracles, Martha & The Vandellas, Jan & Dean, Chubby Checker, Glen Campbell, Jackie Wilson, The Shirelles, The Marvelettes, Bobby Freeman and the list goes on and on.

In 1962, this Guitar found itself recording on a major label—Dot Records. My group became known as The Untouchables.

In 1965, this Guitar, while still touring with literally every major act in the country, found itself with a new label deal and part of a new name. This time it was on a new label (at the time), A&M Records out of Los Angeles, and The Untouchables had become Captain Zoom.

Three singles later in 1967, we signed exclusively to Trident Productions (The Kingston Trio, We Five, etc.), and found yet another new home known as Epic Records and, yeah, you guessed it, another name.

The group, now named West, recorded two albums in Nashville and left the label in 1969 to record a third album for Paramount Records. After the group disbanded and having made many friends in Nashville, I decided that maybe this Guitar was qualified to become successful playing sessions in Nashville.

During the next 10-year period, this Guitar lived in the studios and never played on a publishing demo. Every time it came out of its case, it was to record with people like Bob Dylan, Leonard Cohen, Lester Flatt, Earl Scruggs, Marty Robbins, Johnny Cash, Loudon Wainwright III, Hoyt Axton, Willie Nelson, and the list goes on and on. But wait, I'm getting ahead of myself.

With all of the touring and recording in San Francisco, Los Angeles, Nashville, New York City, London, Paris, etc.—it goes without saying that this Guitar became very accustomed to airports, it always traveled with what was known as "escort service."

This meant that it would be taken to the gate at the boarding lounge and hand-carried to a storage area in the belly of the plane. Once at the point of destination, it would be hand-carried from the plane back to the arrival gate and turned over to me. The backfiring of this escort service is what started the event that, even with the uncountable miles of road and tape behind this Guitar, what a small world it can be.

This escort service worked well until this Guitar was selected to take part in what became known as the New Morning sessions with Bob Dylan. We boarded a non-stop American Air Lines flight from San Francisco to New York City to begin the project, to be recording with greats like Al Cooper (keys), Charlie Daniels (bass), Russ Kunkel (drums), and David Bromberg (acoustic guitar).

Using the escort service as I had many times in the past, I didn't foresee any problems with the flight. As always, I opened the guitar case the moment it was handed back to me in the arrival lounge, my heart sunk at what I saw. The tail piece was broken.

With a flying bridge, this left the strings lying flat along the frets, obviously beyond any kind of self-fix. The only comforting thought was that, since it was Thursday with the sessions not starting until Friday evening, there might be a chance of having it repaired. After all, I had always been told that "you can get anything you want in New York City if you have the money." I would now be pressed to prove this right or wrong.

Once situated at my New York home of the time—the Chelsea Hotel—I immediately set out to find someone to repair the crippled instrument.

Having spent a lot of time in New York City, it didn't take long to decide where to begin my search. I proceeded directly to Manny's, which, by the way, had more guitars than any music store I'd ever been in. Literally hundreds of guitars lined the walls from floor to ceiling. The main showroom was about two stores deep with walls that extended high enough to accommodate two floors. Surely it would be easy in a store of this magnitude to have my Guitar repaired.

At first, the man behind the counter, after looking at my Guitar, seemed optimistic in finding a tail piece for the instrument. As his search went on, his optimism waned and my concern grew for his ability to come through. Over an hour went by with him looking in every book, every drawer and

"I'm playing tomorrow night with Bob Dylan. I simply must get the Guitar fixed."
—Ron Cornelius

every shelf, even going through many of them over and over. Finally, he looked at me and said, "I just don't have it."

By this time he knew how important it was to find this part. I had explained to him I'd come all the way from San Francisco to record with Bob Dylan. His compassion led him to assemble a list of stores in the city that might succeed in helping me. I don't know if he was a player or not, but he clearly understood that another guitar would not do at a time like this.

Knowing that I was facing, in my opinion, the most important two weeks of session work in my career, I had to have my Guitar, the one that had been by my side nearly every day for the past fifteen years. It had become an extension of me, or had I become an extension of it?

After flying, checking in to the hotel, and spending time at Manny's, it now was late in the day on Thursday. I still wasn't too worried about finding the guitar part I needed. After all, I had all the next day and, don't forget, I was in New York City. So, I returned to the Chelsea Hotel and focused on the shrimps in green sauce, the famous paella, and sangria at the Don Quixote restaurant just off and adjoining the lobby.

I had called a few friends to join me for dinner. Among them was Bill Donovan, the tour manager for our tours with Leonard Cohen and Charlie Daniels.

Charlie's career hadn't taken off yet and he was in town to play bass on the upcoming sessions. At that point in time he weighed around 350 pounds, and not only looked funny, but was very funny. Quite frankly, he fell prey to many practical jokes played on him and, not being proud of it now, I was one of the jokesters. This night the joke played on him by me almost got us shot.

While enjoying this fine Spanish cuisine we couldn't help but hear a droning sound coming from over where the bar was located. On one of my trips to the restroom I made it my business to find out what was making this sound that was starting to get on our nerves. I discovered it was a man speaking through a hole in his throat with a battery powered amplifier of some sort. I felt embarrassed, to say the least. However, having had one or two too many glasses of sangria than I should have, I thought of having some fun with Good Old Charlie.

When I returned to our table I told Charlie, in front of everyone, that the man with the voice box was faking. I told him that I had just heard him speaking as plain as anyone and laughing at how his "put on" was annoying our table. Charlie became enraged and set out to go tell off this creep.

Approaching the man, he said, "Get that stupid tube out of your mouth you phony S.O.B. I've listened to that shit as long as I'm going to."

Charlie was serious and the man stepped back. In a blink of an eye, two dark-complexion, expensively-suited men drew guns. As the guns cleared their clothing you could hear the hammers cock. There was no doubt that shots would be quickly forthcoming.

Little did we know that this small man with the voice box was a regular at the bar and was very well liked by the Spanish-owned establishment.

At any rate, I knew my joke had quickly gone too far and I couldn't get into the scene fast enough. This was no time for trying to bullshit anyone—I went straight for the truth. I told the men that Charlie had nothing to do with this joke of clearly bad taste. I explained, I apologized and told them that Charlie was a victim of a cheap shot delivered by me. If they would just allow us to leave quietly, we would be gone and never again cause anything like this to happen in their place.

One of them, being a little less intent on violence, said "Go, now." And we did. Needless to say, my practical joking slowed down immensely after this incident.

The next day started early for me. With the list of music stores the man at Manny's had given me, I hit the streets. The first store was a hole-in-the-wall store that actually specialized in violins, mandolins, cellos, and things of that nature. I felt as though there wasn't much chance of finding what I needed, but I pressed on anyway. It didn't take long to prove my instincts right. No such part existed in the small establishment. The next store I visited looked like pay dirt.

They represented an extensive line of guitars, one of them being Gretsch. Being a family-owned establishment, they also had their own in-house repair shop. It didn't take long for them to locate what they thought was the exact part. Taking my Guitar, they went to work as I gave the waiting cab driver thumbs up.

I knew this job would take a while, so I decided this was a perfect opportunity to grab some lunch. One of the things I long for when I visit New York City is the cabbage soup from the Russian Tea Room. The first time I was told about this place, I was also told to try that soup. My first thought was a soup made from cabbage would certainly not register high on my list, but the person telling me this was so convincing, I figured I'd try it, given the opportunity.

Sure enough, from the first bite I was sold and have never missed a chance to repeat that delightful experience. This particular day, I had one bowl and headed back to, hopefully, pick up the Guitar.

Unfortunately, more bad news was waiting for me at the music store. The repair shop couldn't figure out why a standard part, of which they had several, wouldn't fit this Guitar. When I informed the repair man that Gretsch only made this model by hand during the first year of availability, it cleared up his problem but left me with no tail piece that would fit. Now, I started to panic. Time was running out fast. The sessions were to begin in a few hours and I was no closer than before to getting this Guitar up and running.

Two music stores later with no luck, it was recommended that I try a large store by the name of Manny's. When I informed them I had started my search at Manny's, I was told I should have asked to see the old man who had a repair shop upstairs in the back. I couldn't believe after all of the sincere concern shown by the guy at Manny's, he wouldn't have mentioned anything about this old man. At any rate, I headed back to see if there was any validity to what I'd been told.

The story proved to be true. I hadn't been told about this man because he worked on only acoustic instruments. By this time anything was worth a try, so I asked if I could talk with him.

I was directed back behind the counter to an old stairway with a door at the top. I met the old man and presented him with my problem. He asked to see the Guitar and within a few minutes I had gone to the car and returned with it. He and I stood side by side and with the Guitar on his work bench, I opened the case for his perusal.

While showing him the damage, I had a strange feeling come over me. I could feel this old man staring at me instead of the Guitar. I looked over at him and with a touch of desperation in my voice, I said, "Well, what do you think."

He said, "I think that you don't remember me."

Now I was really confused. I said, "Remember you? From where?"

It was then that my skin started to tingle as he told me he was the man who assembled this Guitar years and years ago when he lived in California and worked for Gretsch. He stopped working for them when Gibson bought the company in 1960. He remembered me as a young boy delighted with the fact of finally owning an instrument of this quality. He remembered me choosing the fastest neck offered at the time. He even remembered how my eyes lit up when he told me about the little gold plaque on the head of the Guitar that would read "For Ron Cornelius—by Gretsch."

While he worked, I told him a lot about what all I had done with this Guitar since it had left his hands back in 1959. Watching him work was like watching a doctor set the broken leg of a teenager he had delivered at birth.

It goes without saying that inside of two hours he had the Guitar up and playing by fashioning a tail piece out of a small block of stainless steel, right there in his shop. It remains on the Guitar to this day and has never given a moment's trouble.

I would venture to say that no guitar's "histography," that I know of, could match the one held by this instrument. Taking into consideration all of its accomplishments as well as the travel its seen, it only goes to show that, even for a guitar, "The World Can Sometimes Be Very Small."

CHAPTER TWO

THE GIFT

At some point in time I was told it takes every turn, every step and every good or bad decision you've ever made to get you exactly where you are today. This has been a truth for me many times in my life. Being caught up in situations that have made me look back and retrace steps in life that led me to a certain place in time is something I've taken a long, appreciative look at on many occasions.

This story is of one of those times and focuses on a personal gift that I received from Bob Dylan one night in New York City. Before I get to the actual gift, I say, "Let's go back."

The force that led me to "The Gift" was that of becoming a session player, and the mounting credentials that led to more prestigious session dates as time went by.

I guess the first session date I played in my life, other than recording demo tapes with my own group, was in the early 60s. An artist by the name of Bobby Freeman was probably the most successful talent in the San Francisco Bay area at that time. He had nationwide success with a record entitled "Do You Wanna Dance." My group, The Untouchables, played the majority of his live shows and we all became friends traveling all over California together.

Another old friend of mine was Sylvester Stewart, later to become famous the world over, as Sly And The Family Stone. At that time, Sly was the featured person in a group by the name of The Continentals.

Two other old friends of mine at that time were Tom Donahue and Bob Mitchell. They were in radio and pretty much pioneered FM Radio as we have known it since that time. They were very influ-ential in the industry and were involved with all of our careers.

The teaming up of Sly as a producer with Bobby Freeman proved to be a winning idea. Sly produced a record on Bobby entitled, "The S-W-I-M," which would be the first time I played on a real record as a hired musician.

My group was under contract at the time and even though we were making records, I welcomed the opportunity to try my hand at this level of musical skill. With the success of the records that were currently out during that time on which I had played and by frequenting Coast Recorders on Bush Street in San Francisco, I was contacted by an ad agency in the city by the name of Campbell/Ewald.

Over the next couple of years my session work turned to commercials. I, along with my group, made commercials for a long string of companies. We performed commercials for every line of jeans that Levi Strauss manufactured. Folger's Coffee was another client who gave us plenty of work, and for the year 1966 we won commercial of the year for our work with Chevrolet. This commercial success brought into the picture a musical instrument company by the name of VOX. Their entrance into the marketplace came through the British Invasion. Groups like the Dave Clark Five and the Beatles brought them fame.

My group was chosen to help pioneer their entrance into the United States. Free of charge, they provided us with guitars, amplifiers, drums, and a slew of all kinds of gear. In return, my group made the first VOX demonstration album for their company.

Some of the equipment we demonstrated, in my opinion at the time, didn't have a chance of being marketable. On most of these opinions, I was wrong.

For instance, I was in possession of the first Wah-Wah pedal to come into the country. This was a variable tone-bender of sorts in the form of a foot pedal. I laughed at this one.

In order to make the demo recording of how it sounded, I had to let a friend hold it in his hand, pushing and pulling the pedal in and out while I played a certain guitar lick while recording it.

Needless to say, it became a very big selling item. Over and above all of the free equipment, we were paid very well for this demonstration series and I still to this day have it and I'm very proud to still have it in my collection.

Soon after that time the Pop Art syndrome came onto the scene. Changing the name of our group to Captain Zoom, we were then signed to A&M Records in Los Angeles and would record three single releases under that name.

With marginal success, this led us to signing a management deal with Trident Productions, owned by a man named Frank Werber in San Francisco. At that time, Trident also represented the Kingston Trio and We Five. Their building, located at the corner of Columbus and Kerney in San Francisco, was later purchased by Frances Ford Copolla. It had a studio in the basement that became a home away from home for us.

On the strength of that relationship and the tapes that we rolled there came our first major label album deal with Epic Records. Our sound had evolved into somewhat of a country-flavored approach. When Clive Davis and Dick Asher signed us to the label, part of our deal was that we would record our music in Nashville, Tennessee.

None of us had ever been there, but somehow it seemed like the place for us to be. Outside of Bob Dylan, no "long hairs" had arrived on the music scene in Nashville before us.

People in the town looked upon us as freaks any time we left our hotel. The still popular Pancake Pantry, owned by a man known at the time as Bigot Bob, was the worst. We only tried to eat there on one occasion. Before we could even take a seat, he yelled from the kitchen area, "OK, little ladies, just turn it around and get it right on out of here. We ain't got a thing here for you."

It was scary in the South for us, but for some reason we needed to lay our music down in Nashville. We always recorded between midnight and daylight; this was also part of our deal.

We had some pretty crazy ideas back then. Another silly idea brought forth was that we wouldn't play sessions for anyone. We never used session players on our records and we somehow picked up the idea that to play sessions for anyone else would be giving away part of our unique sound.

However, during the course of the next two years, I was asked to play on other albums in Nashville and I refused. After one hit single and two albums with Epic, the group, known as West, decided to disband. The single entitled "Just Like Tom Thumbs Blues" was ironically written by Bob Dylan, whom I had never met at the time. This would, of course, prove to be a conversation piece later on.

The breaking up of West was very hard for me. A couple of the members wanted to venture out and do something else. For me it was like the end of a great road that I had been on for a long time. I couldn't understand how they could have worked for so long to finally get a career going like we had, then just quit and walk away from it.

This proved to be an example of how sometimes things that seem to be so bad can actually be the beginning of something very good. I was the one who least wanted to see the group break up. Other than Michael Stewart, out acoustic guitarist, the situation worked out in the long run better for me than for anyone.

Michael immediately went into production with his first project—Billy Joel's first album entitled *Piano Man*. Once the breakup of West and all that goes along with the demise of an organization, that had been together for years was behind me, I was totally open and available as a session player.

I had made many connections in Nashville during the preceding period and soon a few opportunities opened up for me. The first album I had a chance to be involved with was a surprise. The artist was Burl Ives and they needed some simple acoustic work added to the already recorded master.

I got quite a kick out of this because as a child I loved his song "Jimmy Crack Com." As a little boy, I would go around singing this song and now as an adult to be involved with his music was great.

Next came the first series of sessions I would play in the studio with other musicians, recording a full album with Lester Flatt and Earl Scruggs. This was very exciting for me because to get in there with these boys I knew that I would have to come to the table with real Country guitar work.

They were riding high with the success of the motion picture sound track from Bonnie & Clyde, and Columbia Records was going all out for them. I knew that most of the musicians would be from Lester and Earl's group, the Foggy Mountain Boys, and, to the best of my memory, the only outside players to be hired were myself and Kenny Buttrey, whom I knew to be a very fast lane session man at the time.

Being saddled up with players like Roland White (mandolin) and Josh Graves (dobro) would be a new height of accomplishment for me.

To put into context how important these sessions were to me, I want to point out a sacrifice that I had to make in order to take part. I always wanted to go to Europe by way of ship. A couple of months earlier, a friend and I purchased passage on the *QE II*, which would take us from New York to London. We had already received our tickets which had arrived in leather cases with our names embossed in gold leaf print. I canceled the entire trip in order to attend the Nashville sessions.

I left San Francisco and showed up in Nashville the day before the session date only to find out that Lester had taken sick. The sessions were postponed and the album had been put back a month. It was too late to rebook the trip abroad. Unfortunately, to this day, I've never taken the time to make the cruise.

Later when the sessions were rescheduled, I returned to Nashville to find Lester in good health and ready to go.

On the first day, while in the middle of a take, Lester observed a pass that I was into and nodded saying, "Oh, yeah." His acknowledgment of my ability shot a hole right through any apprehensions that I may have had about being able to hang with these players.

The album took about two weeks to record and from that moment on I had no problems. Kenny Buttrey and I played on this album and one more with Lester and Earl. They would be the last two albums that Lester and Earl would make after 32 years of being together.

An interesting involvement happened after Lester and Earl parted ways. Kenny and I played on the very first album that Earl ever made without Lester, and we also played on the very first album that Lester ever made without Earl. For some reason I enjoy knowing that, even though timing is the only thing responsible for it.

Later on I played on the Earl Scruggs 25 anniversary album when Earl completed 25 years with Columbia Records. This album included Billy Joel, Loggins and Messina, Carl Perkins, Charlie Daniels, and an array of artists who came out of the woodwork to take part in the tribute.

It wasn't long until I was enjoying all of the session work that I wanted. For 12 years I worked on over 150 albums and during that period never played on one publishing demo.

Every time tape was rolled with me in place it was to be all major label releases. Having accomplished all that I could hope for, as a session player, I'll always be grateful for the first major calls I received. These albums were the ones that started my phone ringing on a continuous basis.

One thing that became clear to me early on was that I felt drawn to artists who were using their music to speak to the people. Curiously, they were usually not the best singers. Nor were they so concerned with the commercial aspect of music, but were driven toward getting things said in a way that could make a difference.

For instance, when I went to the prison in California for the making of Johnny Cash's album *Live At San Quentin*, it was obvious Cash had earned the right and had the ability to speak to the man with calluses on his hands, heart, and soul. He

The line-up would be:

Bob Dylan, acoustic guitar
Charlie Daniels, bass
Russ Kunkel, drums
David Bromberg, acoustic guitar
Al Kooper, keys
Me, electric guitar

could identify with the man who desperately wanted to turn his life around and it showed in his music.

The night I played some acoustic guitar parts on Marty Robbins' "My Woman, My Woman, My Wife," I knew the man could speak big-time to the relationship between a man and a woman.

When recording the album *Attempted Mustache* with Loudon Wainwright III, it didn't take a mental gymnast to know that this guy had the attention of intellectuals nationwide. He not only was very funny, his songs made us laugh in a thought-provoking way.

And playing on five albums with Leonard Cohen ... please! His sheer control of language that spoke to the hidden characters of the heart and mind always left me in awe.

My guitar work can be found on five Bob Dylan albums. He being the spokesman for an entire generation, it was a special goal to record with him and I had my sights set on that goal for a long time.

The first Dylan album I was asked to play on was recorded in Nashville and was entitled *Self Portrait*. This album had a string of players a mile long and, though I was grateful for the call, I longed to record with Dylan in a more intimate musical atmosphere.

I was quoted as saying that "I would walk from San Francisco to New York" to make such an album.

In fact, when Bob Johnston (Dylan's producer at the time) called me at my home in California, he asked if I remembered making that statement.

Of course, I said, "Yes!"

He replied, "Well, start walking. We're cutting in two weeks."

The line-up would be Dylan playing acoustic guitar, Charlie Daniels playing bass, Russ Kunkel on drums, David Bromberg on acoustic guitar, Al Kooper on keys, and me on electric guitar with perhaps some work from George Harrison.

For the next week and a half I thought of nothing but the upcoming sessions. I knew there would be no way of finding out what songs we would record beforehand in order to work out anything. This would be a go-for-what-you-know-right-here-right-now situation.

It seemed like forever getting through that week, but finally the day of departure came and I headed for the airport. I left San Francisco early on Thursday with the sessions to begin the following evening.

Musically getting started with this project, which would become known as the *New Morning* sessions, was like taking a ride on a Chinese tiger. To begin with, there was no ending to the amount of songs flying around in Dylan's head. The waterfall of material pouring out at us was constant and overwhelming, to say the least.

Many times during the next two weeks my old friend Charlie Daniels and I would look at each other, shake our heads in amazement, and then quickly resume the concentration level needed to stay aboard.

Even though I'd recorded many albums prior to this one, Dylan's song-by-song approach was nothing like I'd been around and took getting used to. Each time we were exposed to a new song, he'd stand there and play it through for us. Once we had our charts together and had kicked it around a bit, it was time to red light the song and put it down.

At that point he would count the song off in a completely different tempo than we'd just rehearsed it. This would, of course, put us all in a crazy place but with the level of players in the room and charts in front of us, we fired away at his newly presented target.

We had to get used to expecting the unexpected, but then again, "What did we expect?"

During the first pass of a song, if anyone fell off badly he would say, "Let's take it again."

Then he would count the same song off in another completely different tempo than we had just recorded. I'm not just talking basic tempo, either. He might change it rhythmically as well—you just had to be ready for anything.

If anyone fell off badly on the second take, he would say, "Let's take it again," at which time he'd pull the same stunt on us.

If we didn't get it right during one of those three takes he'd say, "Next song," and that was the end of that.

Even with our charts, he kept us in uncharted territory which, speaking for myself, kept pulling out spontaneous musical responses that would not have occurred otherwise. Needless to say, we had to keep our chins down and our lefts up in order to hang in there.

Being mentally exhausted at the end of the day was a given, but without rehearsing parts we were just playing music and having a great time.

"You're giving a hundred and ten percent to this one, and I really appreciate it."
—Bob Dylan

(After we had rolled on for over a week, the song "New Morning" popped up. This song would be the catalyst between me and Dylan, and the gift that entitles this story.)

While in the control room of the studio listening to the play-back of this song, Dylan looked at me when my solo came by and said, "Yeah, man!"

Before moving on to the next song he came to me and said, "Ya know, I've noticed how hard you've been working on this album. You're giving a hundred and ten percent to this one, and I really appreciate it. I know you're getting paid well, but is there anything else I can do for you other than that?"

After taking a moment I said, "Let me think about that."

I knew by the way he talked that he meant what he said and I figured I would either ask for something really nice or ask for nothing at all.

After some time had passed I told him I had decided what I wanted from him. He said, "Name it."

Knowing that the sessions would be ending at 6:00 PM on Friday, I asked if he would hang around after everyone left so we could be alone in the studio. He looked at me as if I were a little weird, and I didn't blame him, but he agreed.

Friday came and at the end of the day we waited and waited. When everyone had finally left the control room he said, "OK, Ron, what's it gonna be?"

I told him that I had really enjoyed the last two weeks working on the album and if he really wanted to give me a gift, I wanted him to grab his guitar and come out into the main room of the studio.

Once there, I said, "For my gift, I want you to sit down at the piano with your guitar on your lap."

I then explained to him that I wanted to lie down next to the piano with a pillow under my head and start spouting off requests of my all-time favorite Dylan songs. If he wrote a certain song on the piano, then I wanted him to play the piano while he sang, and if he wrote it on the guitar, play the guitar.

I started way back early in his career and worked on toward the present. Once I had heard enough of a certain song I would clap my hands and request another title.

So, for about 30 minutes I lay there on the floor of that old, dark CBS studio in New York City, clapping my hands and spouting off titles.

It was my own private Bob Dylan concert, and, without a doubt, one of the nicest gifts anyone has ever given me.

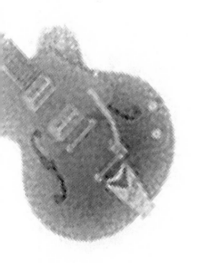

CHAPTER THREE

JERUSALEM

It was a light, breezy summer day when we landed at the Lod International Airport in Israel. My crew (the singers and musicians known as "The Army" traveling with Leonard Cohen), seemed unusually quiet at the time, after much conversation regarding the machine gun killings by terrorists that had transpired just a few days prior to our arrival. One of our people still had the front page newspaper clippings showing the bodies of victims who fell in the terminal lobby exactly where we stood. In the pictures were musical instruments strewn around, bringing to mind that we could very easily have been among these unfortunates had our tour been one week shorter.

It was a four-month concert tour that started on St. Patrick's Day in Dublin, Ireland, and ended in Jerusalem. We were scheduled to play two concerts this particular week, the first being in Tel Aviv and the second in Jerusalem.

With the windows down on our ride from the airport to Tel Aviv, the orange blossoms seemed to take away some of the uneasiness that cloaked the afternoon. It was pointed out that the beautiful orchards on both sides of our view were nothing but wasteland just a few years back.

Prior to the Six-Day War between the Arabs and the Israelis, the land that we were now seeing was Arab territory and totally undeveloped. It was amazing what the Israelis had done with it once it became theirs. In my childhood days, having spent quite a lot of time in the San Joaquin valley of California, I thought I knew what neatly manicured orchards looked like. The blossoming groves in the memory of my youth didn't compare to the heavenly horticulture on display as we rolled on toward Tel Aviv.

Once in our hotel rooms and comfortable, we began our usual get-acquainted-with-the-food-and-drink of whatever country we were in, and my constant companions of that time—Cognac and Hashish—rounded out the afternoon quite nicely. As evening took over we could see the lights of Jerusalem.

Even though we'd played concerts in countries all over the world many times, I felt different here. I didn't know why I felt that way, I just knew I did. That evening I ended up with Leonard in a small town by the name of Jafa in the home of an old friend of his. I don't remember the man's name, but I will never forget his art. His paintings and sculpture made me feel like beauty was in this man's hands and from now on I could forget "the eye of the beholder." Words were out of place in the presence of such astonishing works, and silence was the only applicable offering that would come from me that night.

I saw legs broken, heads bashed in, and arms of beautiful young Israeli girls twisted until they actually broke before my eyes.

We drank untold amounts of Ouzo and ate delicious breads with hummus, and without noticing, most of the night was gone and morning wasn't far off. Upon arriving back at my hotel, I could only feel full appreciation for this evening of growth and enlightenment. I stopped at the hotel lounge, had one more cognac and went to bed—alone.

The next day was full of surprises. As a rule, we only performed at glorious venues such as The Royal Albert Hall in London, The Vienna Opera House in Austria, Tivoli Gardens in Copenhagen, or The Olympia Theatre in Paris, France. By contrast, tonight's show would be held in a gymnasium here in Tel Aviv.

The acoustics in the gymnasium were atrocious and to make things worse, the floor had just been freshly re-lacquered. At sound check, the officials made it very clear there would be no seating on the main floor, forcing everyone to be seated on the sides in the bleachers or at the complete opposite end from the stage. We were explicitly warned that all hell would break loose should anyone touch their precious new floor.

That night during our show, Leonard decided that he wasn't getting to the crowd with the out-of-touch seating arrangement to which we were subjected. He then invited the entire audience to come down from their seats onto the main floor and just as we'd been warned, all hell did break loose.

With the onslaught of a regiment of orange-coated security, a violent exhibition of force took place. I saw legs broken, heads bashed in, and arms of beautiful young Israeli girls twisted until they actually broke before my eyes. These bastards were ruthless and seemed to be enjoying what they were doing.

The concert ended at that moment and we were lucky to get out of there without losing someone. My anger was uncontrollable. To understand how anyone could do these things to fans who merely came to enjoy an evening of music was completely beyond me.

Needless to say, we slept very little that night. I had the empty feeling, in part, of being responsible for something bad that could and should have been avoided. I was outwardly angry and inwardly ashamed. I wasn't the one who started things off, but not being able to stop it left me feeling ineffective, to say the least.

The next day a couple of friends and I ventured out to the city of Jerusalem. We spent most of the day walking through the streets and absorbing the everyday ongoings of a culture very foreign to me. I sat for long periods in dirt-floor tea rooms and shared opium palates with street people; people, no doubt, I should have had better sense than to associate with. I found myself surrounded by an air of low regard for any human life, much less my own.

At one point I found myself staring down a series of brick steps that led onto a huge rock floor area stopping abruptly at the Wailing Wall. This area was crowded with Jewish people ritualistically jumping up and down, sticking notes in the mortar cracks of the wall, and consumed in prayer. You can bet that I did not set foot onto the rock-floored area, as full-blown respect turned me back.

Later, I left the city to find Bethlehem, not only see the route that Mary and Joseph took on their journey, but to locate, if I could, the actual manger spot of the birthplace of Jesus. I was surprised that a Greek Orthodox church had been built on that spot, but took comfort when informed that in the basement of the church I could still reach the so-called place of birth. Upon entering the church, I noticed many incense burners hung by chains from the ceiling, partially filling the room with thick, aromatic clouds. After walking to the rear of the sanctuary, I descended two small flights of stairs.

Once there, I found a small opening that resembled a fireplace with a metal star on the floor which was well back in the opening. In the center of the star, a flame burned with quiet brilliance. This was the birthplace I sought. As my luck sometimes runs, this occasion took an unavoidable left turn.

An old woman, I'm going to guess 85 or 90 in years and obviously out of her mind, began screaming and crying while trying to crawl into the opening with the flame. She, of course, was not delivering her pain in English, but it didn't take a mental gymnast to understand that she was hurting as though Jesus had just been crucified this morning.

She had to be bodily removed from the place and, believe me, she didn't go quietly. It was very disturbing and being witness to her agony made me wonder why this had to go down at this precise point in time. My senses were standing on end when I left the church.

Soon I was in route back to Tel Aviv, focused on quickly getting to my hotel room. I needed to be alone. I needed to reflect on the day and try to recoup some order to my thoughts. The evening came and went without incident and, quite frankly, I welcomed the chance just to be still.

Directly across from the Java Gate in Jerusalem stands a beautiful concert house. It blends in with the earthy surroundings, as do all buildings in the area, made with the sand and mortar from the ground it stands on. This was to be the site of our concert in Jerusalem scheduled for that night.

Once inside, we could tell that this would be a great place to play. Trying to put the ordeal of the preceding concert behind us, we were determined not to let it affect our delivery in this great place. After a very easy sound check, we retired to our staging area and spent the next couple of hours readying ourselves for the show. Several times before the concert, I left our backstage area to look at the crowd. I remember taking note of the quietness of the audience.

The place was completely sold out and it seemed unusual for this many people to be nearly totally quiet. When it came time to actually take the stage for our show we were all taken aback by the silence. The concentrated attention of the audience on our every move was noticeably different from the usual concert crowd. As was our normal program approach, we played one hour and then announced our intermission of 30 minutes. To that point the show had gone wonderfully and we were all pleased with the performance level.

During the break while discussing our next set with Leonard, we were interrupted by our tour manager, Bill Donovan. He told Leonard that a security guard wanted to speak with him. Leonard asked me if I would mind handling this and I agreed. Outside our door I was confronted with a very large guard dressed in a uniform resembling as SS storm trooper in style.

His English was very broken, but he was finally able to convey that when we took the stage to resume our concert, the audience would like to sing us a song. What I thought he was saying was someone from the audience wanted to sing a song. I told him we couldn't allow anyone to come on stage during our show. He pressed on, saying, "No, I meant just what I said. The audience would like to sing to you."

I relayed this message to Leonard, so when we took the stage from our break, we all assumed an Indian style sitting position in a semi-circle facing the audience, and waited.

After sitting for a few minutes, a song began to break out in the audience. At first the sound came from different areas of the house, but soon the voices lowed together and the entire audience was singing to us. What a special moment it was as they gave us this incomparable gift of a traditional Hebrew song entitled, "I Bring You Peace."

At one point, crazy as it sounds, I actually laid face down on the ground with my arms and legs spread out as far apart as possible. I just wanted to hold on to the ground for some reason.

As this song filled the air, the effect it had on me was tremendous. Immediately a different melody than being sang came into my head, simultaneously joined by a lyric response to the magical offering from the audience.

Concerned that I might lose what I had in mind, I reached behind me and took up the guitar. Leaning over to the musician next to me (David O'Conner), I played through the melody, drafting him to help me remember exactly how it went in hopes of recalling it later.

Over half of the new song (lyric and melody) was finished in a matter of seconds, right there on stage, and were never changed in any way. I finished the song on the Greek island of Hydra where I spent time after the tour. The song, entitled "Jerusalem," was later recorded and released by Esther Ofarim and The London Philharmonic Orchestra. It was again recorded live in concert and released by Esther Ofarim and the Tel Aviv Symphony.

What a great honor to have such a wonderful lady record this song. The live album was further testament that the song was a divinely inspired gift to me. Most of the songs on the album were traditional two-thousand-year-old Hebrew songs, but only a couple, including my song "Jerusalem," were new.

Jerusalem Sang To Me One Night
Made Me Feel As Light
As Any Star Is Bright
She Sang I Bring You Peace

Once the concert was over, we were invited to dinner in a small upstairs restaurant in Jerusalem which led the evening on and out into a cerebral spiral of unexplainability. I was the last to arrive and upon entering the dining room was taken aback by what I saw. The waiters serving the food were none other than the orange-coated security guards who we had encountered two nights back in Tel Aviv.

Let me stop and repeat this! No, they were not men who reminded me of the security guards— they were the exact same bastards, serving the food and being friendly as though they'd never met our group before. Just a short time ago we were at the concert hall in a wonderfully special space in time, and now we were in some Felini type nightmare.

I hit the door and never had an urge to look back.

After walking for a short while, our tour manager, Bill Donovan, caught up to inform me that our cars back to Tel Aviv would be leaving soon. He was very concerned when I told him I wouldn't be returning with them that night. I told him to go on with the others and I would see them all at the hotel the next day. He thought I was crazy to chance the night in the dark streets of Jerusalem alone. But if I had allowed him to convince me to come back, I would have missed the oncoming event to which this whole story has been leading.

The last of a grueling four-month tour, the last few days in Israel and, yes, the last few hours had all mounted up to a point which far surpassed concern for my personal safety. It didn't cross my mind for a moment as I walked and walked in the coldness of that night that I might be in danger. I felt no need for companionship. Each step I took seemed more in place than ever before. It was a strange sensation, but every time my foot went down, it was like a magnet had placed it exactly where it should be.

At one point, crazy as it sounds, I actually laid face down on the ground with my arms and legs spread out as far apart as possible. I just wanted to hold on to the ground for some reason.

With all that was spinning wildly in my mind, laced on all sides by the new song relentlessly playing on and on in my head, it was a comforting sight when, off to the right, I noticed the moon in full glory. I was very cold and I remember thinking I was looking at the same moon the people back home were looking at. It was at that moment my heart nearly stopped.

There, looking off to my left, also was the moon in full glory. Looking immediately back to my right, I confirmed it for myself. The moon was to the right and also to the left. Yes, there were two moons in the sky over Jerusalem that night. Obviously having a big-time problem with what I was seeing, I wondered if my brain had in some way short circuited under the confusion and pressure of the last few days.

On one hand I was experiencing fear, but on the other there was a strange sort of peacefulness about me. Things were all wrong, but it was all right. The vividness of that event will be with me if I live to be 200 years old. It was the bright feeling of a once-in-lifetime thing to witness.

As I walked on, I came to a cobblestone bridge that arched over whatever was beneath. Walking toward me in the dimly lit, misty late hour was a couple. Arm in arm, they seemed to be warming each other.

I welcomed the sight as I saw an opportunity to validate the extraordinary sky display. I walked straight up to them and stopped them as they were halfway down the bridge and told them I meant them no harm, but I needed some help.

Quickly it became evident that the female spoke no English. The man spoke only a little English, but enough that I felt he could be of some help. I asked if they could see the moon as I pointed to one of them.

His reply was, "Yes, of course."

I then asked if he could see the other moon in the opposite direction.

Likewise his report was, "Yes."

In the presence of another human, the situation suddenly became rather emotional. Wiping back a few escaping tears I said, "How can this possibly be?"

His answer was like a warm, enveloping blanket of comfort to me. Before walking on he looked me directly in the eyes and said, "Young man, it's clear to me that you don't know where you are."

I knew immediately what he meant.

I was in the city of miracles—Jerusalem.

CHAPTER FOUR

MENTAL MAGIC

It's always amazed me how music can administer this thing called "relief." To the healthy mind, it can be as simple as temporarily lessening sadness by invoking nostalgia and the remembrance of happier times. To a deeply disturbed mind, it can sometimes bring to the surface responses that doctors, medicines and tons of therapy have not been able to touch.

Concert tours with Leonard Cohen were always very comfortable. We traveled only by air, usually having three days in each city. In three days' time we could usually get a pretty good feel of what was musically happening and find clubs that provided late night jam sessions—anything to play a little more music.

At some point in time we decided to use our days off to do something as a group in addition to the scheduled concerts. For the better part of a year, all throughout the United States, Canada, and the entire European continent, we took our music to insane asylums. I watched the effects it had on many different occasions.

I now look back on all of those outings with a great deal of pleasure. However, I must admit when the idea was first brought up, I was the one person in our musical family who was dead against it. The very thought of going into those places scared me and, at first, I flat refused to go.

After a few days of contemplation and many discussions with Leonard and our group about what this venture could mean to a lot of unfortunate people, I agreed to try it a couple of times on the grounds that if I could not get comfortable with it, I would stop.

From that point on it wasn't long until I was ashamed when remembering some of the things I had said regarding these institutions and actually began looking forward to going—any time, any place.

The first outing was a most interesting experience. We left the Mayfair Hotel in three Daimler limousines to play at a very large institution located about two hours to the north of London. The drive was a quiet one for me and I questioned myself as to how, just a couple of nights ago, I could walk out on the stage of the sold out Royal Albert Hall with no butter-flies in my stomach and at this moment it was in knots.

As we finally drove onto the grounds of this ancient institu-tion sitting alone out in the English countryside, I became depressed taking in the visual. The high walls surrounding the place reminded me of some old prison from the Dark Ages. My mind slipped back to the day I attended the making of Johnny Cash's *Live At San Quentin* album and was told that many of the prisoners there were just sick in the mind.

I had grown up just across the bay from the prison and had acquaintances doing time there and, quite frankly, I didn't see them as sick. The real difference I saw between them and the rest of society, in my opinion, was most of us consider the consequences of an act before committing it. These guys just do it before the consequences come into their mind. I've always looked at that as something beyond my understanding.

Anyway, once inside this old asylum we were taken to a very large, sterile room to wait until the administrative staff was ready for us. We were informed that our concert would take place in the cafeteria and at the proper time a group of orderlies would escort us across the grounds. They seemed apprehensive about us having any contact with their patients and this elevated my anxiety.

When we finally arrived at the location of where we were to perform, it was easy to see that the room was originally an auditorium, now doubling as a cafeteria. It had a proper stage at one end of the room and while readying our stage set up, we began encountering a few patients who came in ahead of the main body that would be in attendance.

One young man looked to be around 25 years old and was very glad to see us. He was born with a piece of his scull missing. The triangular shaped hole openly exposed the membrane that covers the brain and he delighted in going from person to person saying, "See? See?"

Well, I could see, and this was all I needed at that moment. My comfort level was descending rapidly.

Soon an orderly removed him from the stage and located him in a seat out front as the room was filling up with approximately 300 patients. They were all wearing white gowns, giving off the appearance of some medieval cuckoo's nest.

There was a diverse spectrum of behavior in the crowd that night. They had every area covered. Some were going stark raving wild, while 17 patients sitting side by side in the front row would not even blink. I was told they were catatonic and never moved.

Soon it was time to begin. Everyone was forcibly quieted by several big, fat women nurses that made Nurse Ratchet look like Snow White. A few short minutes before we started, the last of the audience entered.

I counted nine in all who filed in, one in front of the other, all holding hands. They were seated in the rear of the room, obviously on purpose and for reasons unknown to me. Their white-gowned attire gave off the hit of some sort of chain gang of insomniacs.

The descriptions I've been using may sound a bit insensitive. My reason for using them is this is the way I felt at the time, though I'm not proud of that at this point in my life.

To my surprise, my mind and heart began to change with one sweet, fell swoop delivered from none other than the young man with the missing scull piece. We had only played two or three songs when right in the middle of a song the young man stood up from his center of the room seat. He started shouting at the top of his voice, "Hold it! Hold it! Stop the music!"

His seat location, being in the center of the isle, made it impossible for the floor orderlies to contain him. Soon we were no longer able to continue the song over his shouting and our song ground to a halt.

With that, still at the top of his voice, he pressed on with his interruption. He said, "OK, OK, OK, you people come here with your music. You have the nice clothes, you have the pretty background singers and shiny instruments. Well, what about me? What do you people really think about me?"

With that he became silent and waited for a response from us. We had no choice but to follow Leonard from the stage and, one by one, make our way personally toward him. He received a sincere hug from all seven of us.

From that moment on, the evening became an enlightening experience as our music took on a therapeutic value that I had no idea existed. This young man had, with his piercing sincerity, drastically reduced this all-important, career-driven entourage of ours down to equal or lesser importance than his own tormented presence.

After a short while, we resumed the music only to observe others now doing things to draw attention personally to themselves. Each time this happened, they received praise from us rather than the punishment normally delivered in this God-forsaken place.

One patient threw her white gown up in the air and began running up and down the aisles in a wonderful display of freedom. Needless to say, others joined her, eager to claim a short period of release.

The nine people in the rear who were led in holding hands all shit their pants at exactly the same moment. They were then led out of the building and were all crying the last time I saw them. I hoped they were not punished for trying to bring attention to themselves in a way that was disgustingly unacceptable to the orderlies who governed them.

All in all, as the evening passed, I lost touch with who affected who the most. Was it us affecting them, or them us? At one time or another that night I cried, laughed, got angry and, remember, I started out a little afraid to even be there.

All of my emotions were triggered and, to say it like it really was, I had feelings that night that I have no words for. Feelings deeply loaded with human concern drafted me to a level of enthusiasm about going to places like this and have never left me. Quite a turn around, I'd say, to have this happen all in the course of one evening.

The mental institutions differed greatly from one to another. To see how countries around the world look upon and treat their mentally handicapped citizens is a real eye opener.

Here in the United States it's a hospital environment, while other countries I've been in are hopelessly lost in the past and offer nothing more than incarceration. One thing that never ceased to amaze me and kept running through these places like an unending thread was how far out the human mind can get when left unattended. Things people would say or write down were, at times, unexplainable and shattering. Sometimes not what the words said as much as how they made me feel.

To my surprise, my mind and heart began to change with one sweet, fell swoop delivered from none other than the young man with the missing scull piece.

Ya see, feelings are all some people have in certain situations and many times, I must admit, the feeling of their words was more understandable than the meaning.

For instance, one very cold night in the north of France we had a hard time finding the asylum we had on our schedule. We were over two hours late and when we finally found it, there was no one to meet us at the front gate. There were several buildings on the property, all looking like something out of a Frankenstein movie. They were all dark except one, which seemed to have some lights on at the top of a long, very wide, stone stairway.

I went up these stairs alone to see if I might find someone who could tell us where we should be. I was freezing by the time I reached the huge wooden doors at the top and quickly drew one back and stepped inside. I now stood there in a colossal reception area with graffiti all over the walls and ceiling.

Not finding anyone to speak with and being too cold to go right back out, I began to read the graffiti. Of course, there were the "fuck you's" and the "fascist something-or-other's," along with the "suck this" or "suck that" that you would expect, but my eye went immediately to one phrase.

I could tell it had obviously been written in rage by the violent, six inch wide, paint brush thrashings. It was also blood red and simply said:

"I HATE B I R T H"

The feeling this visual gave me far surpassed the actual meaning of the words. I was chilled to the bone and, believe me, not from the temperature.

Another example is when words are assembled that really have no literal meaning yet are somehow able to evoke feelings. For instance, we played an asylum in Canada that, for the most part, specialized in patients under 25 years of age. They dealt mainly in drug casualties, abused youths, and, of course, a wide spectrum of problems with young people which manifest themselves in many different ways.

As we played through the evening, I noticed a young man dancing alone to almost every song. The way he danced was very impressive. This was no dance anyone could have taught him. He simply had more natural rhythmic moves than I had ever seen. He, himself, also seemed surprised by his abilities in doing something he didn't know he could do. It was sort of a rhythm/groove/roller coaster type thing.

Toward the middle of our last song he danced over close to the stage adjacent to where I was. With a long sweeping gesture he reached out and stuck something in my boot. I had both hands full of guitar and, therefore, couldn't look to see what it was right then.

After we finished the song I reached into my boot and pulled out a torn off matchbook cover and noticed that he had written something on the inside. I stuffed it into my pocket to read later.

I didn't think of it anymore until much later back at our hotel. While telling someone about the naturally gifted dancer I'd seen, I remembered the matchbook cover. Pulling it out I read his poetic ensemble of words that, as I said, gave me feeling over meaning.

It read, and I quote:

"NOWHERE - LOW ASS - CAN'T BE SEEN DRY DAY - BLACK MATCH NECKLACE QUEEN"

CHAPTER FIVE

THE WHEEL OF CONTROL

This story begins in Paris in the month of April. Needless to say, you couldn't ask for a more beautiful time of year to be in France—I was there to play a concert with Leonard Cohen and had arrived three days early to enjoy some time on my own. I was excited about this concert as it would be held in the Olympia Theater. The Olympia had been closed and this would be the reopening, since Edith Piaf sang at its closing years earlier.

I had taken lodging at the Prince DeGalle Hotel just off of the Champs-Elysees very near the Arc de Triomphe. I had rented a very fast motorcycle in order not to deal with the rudeness of the taxi drivers, having encountered them on previous visits to the city. I loved being able to rip through the city, weaving in and out of traffic, not worrying about anything except the John Darms (gens d'armes, the policemen) on street corners who would threaten to take me down with their capes as I steamed past them a little too fast for their comfort.

From the Louvre to the Eiffel Tower and from the Notre Dame Cathedral to the Place Pigalle—that motorcycle and I were quite a team.

On the afternoon of the concert, I was informed that the limousines were out front ready to take me and a few others over to the theatre for sound check.

Upon arriving, and once inside, I was confronted with a comforting experience. The acoustics of the place were incredible. You could actually stand in the last row of the top balcony and someone standing center stage, with no micro-phone, could whisper and be perfectly understood. This was to play a part in our upcoming performance in a way that was very impressive, although we had no way of knowing it at the time.

After sound check, which took less than an hour in this wonderful room, I returned to the Prince DeGalle, ordered a bottle of cognac sent to my lavish room, and began preparing for a great evening. I had left Anne Drews (another story) at the Mayfair Hotel in London for a week while I went to knock out the part of this tour that went into France.

With enough time for dinner before the start of our 9:30 PM show, I set out with a couple of friends to enjoy a great meal at my favorite restaurant in Paris. When facing the Notre Dame Cathedral, the river Seine borders the right side and on the left, a very narrow little street. On this street about halfway down the long block is a tiny little bar/restaurant called Les Vieux.

Being fortunate to have eaten in fine places the world over, I must say that if that night had been my last meal, and I had to choose the place, it would—no doubt—have been this small unpretentious establishment. After my usual order of escargot, onion soup, and the most incredible Chateau Brian Glasse, not to mention a fine bottle of wine, I sipped a couple of cognacs and took off for the Olympia.

Our arrival at the theatre was uneventful. The place was sold out and, musically, the first show went smoothly. The second half of our performance was just underway when the whole P.A. system went down. It, of course, blew right in the middle of a song and our unit was forced to a grinding halt. After some time, it was related to us there was nothing that could be done.

Had we been in a different venue the concert would, no doubt, have ended at that point. The only amplified instruments on stage were the bass, being played by Charlie Daniels, and my guitar.

So, in remembering our sound check and how wonderful the acoustics had proven to be, Leonard announced to the crowd that if everyone could stay absolutely quiet, we would be able to continue. In a matter of moments you could actually hear a pin drop and very intimately we executed the rest of our show.

To be able to conform to and musically address the original intent of this venue was exceptionally gratifying. After three standing ovations and two encores, Leonard said good night to the audience and we retired to the backstage area.

On our route to the dressing rooms we encountered a group of people. At the center of this group stood a man handsomely dressed with his overcoat draped over his shoulders like a cape. It turned out they were French Diplomats and the man in the center was Minister of Finance with the French government.

I was later informed that this would be the equivalent of the Vice President greeting us if we were in the United States. His conversation with Leonard was in French, but I was able to somewhat decipher it. After many compliments to Leonard concerning his writing and, of course, the evening's performance, he reached from behind and handed Leonard a gift. It was a black, totally opaque glass bottle of Napoleon cognac dating back over a hundred years.

Leonard sincerely thanked him and with full appreciation for the gift, he informed the man that we only had one member of our group who could truly appreciate it.

With that, he turned to me and said, "This obviously belongs to you, Ron."

I could have fallen to the floor because I'd only heard about this stuff. Leonard was right. No one would have been a more appropriate candidate than I, due to my love for cognac.

Later, back at the Prince DeGalle, I sat out on the balcony of my room overlooking the Parisian streets below with two very dear friends and until daylight we slowly tiptoed through this entire bottle of liquid perfection. I will never forget this special treat—and yes, it was that good.

The following day our plane was scheduled to leave Orly Airport around 11:00 AM.

We were booked to headline an outdoor festival with 50,000 people in attendance. The festival was being held about 25 miles inland from Marseilles between Aix-en-Provence and Callas. A lot of gear had been rented in order for us to deliver our show in an outdoor arena so, quite naturally, the crew would be driving in a truck with the equipment. We would fly from Paris to Marseilles, drive on over to the small town of Callas and be there when the equipment and crew arrived.

At breakfast I was told that during the previous evening one of our crew members had fallen completely out over a young Parisian girl and wanted to take her with us on to the next show. Knowing we had an extra seat on the plane since Anne was not with me, I offered my seat and the extra to our crew member and his new girlfriend. This meant that I'd have an eight-hour ride with the equipment, but I wanted to give my seats as a gift.

Besides, it wouldn't hurt me to do a little physical work for a change. Riding with the equipment reminded me of the days when my group was on low-budget club tours in California. In fact, the scenery from Paris to Marseilles reminded me of driving from San Francisco to Los Angeles along Highway One with the ocean on the right and the French countryside on the left. The Mediterranean was noticeably bluer than the Pacific and the water looked inviting. However, when stopping to give that a whirl, it didn't take long for the frigid water to send us back to the truck.

Later that evening we pulled into Marseilles and after leaving a few citizens falling down laughing at my inability to speak their language, we had acquired directions that would take us about 25 miles inland to the small town of Callas where we would rejoin the troop.

Our final destination was a quaint hotel by the name of Auberge. We found it easily, as there were only about six buildings in the entire town square. After checking in and getting squared away, we enjoyed a great get-together dinner with everyone that lasted at least two hours. The food was outstanding and the amount of libations consumed by us was easily enough to qualify as too much.

Sometime around midnight I was informed that the festival site we were scheduled to play the following evening was only about three miles from Callas. I was roaring by that time and consequently decided to drive out to see what it looked like. The festival had already been in full swing for two days and, reportedly, there were over 40,000 people in attendance.

I convinced Charlie Daniels and Bill Donovan, our tour manager, to go with me. Even though Bill didn't think that it was such a good idea for me to drive, I argued until he gave in.

I convinced Charlie Daniels and Bill Donovan, our tour manager, to go with me. Even though Bill didn't think that it was such a good idea for me to drive, I argued until he gave in. The three of us set out with me at the wheel on what would prove to be a once-in-a-lifetime ride. This ride, without Divine Intervention, would have been a devastating experience; and therein lies the reason for this story.

In order to get the full impact of what was about to transpire, you must visualize the route from Callas to the festival. Upon leaving the little town square, the two-lane country road was as straight as an arrow for approximately three miles. Traveling down the road, off to our left, we could see the glow of the festival against the star-filled night sky. At the end of the road was a stop sign. Then we were to turn left, very sharply, almost making a U-turn which would lead us back toward the site.

About a mile prior to arriving at the impending stop sign, the thought crossed my mind that I could drive this car across the open field to my left and cut straight over to the festival site without going all the way to the stop sign and then all the way back along the proper entrance road.

With that in mind, I spun the wheel to the left, jumping over the ditch on the left side of the road, and began speeding across the open field, dirt flying. With Charlie and Bill screaming for me to stop, I put the throttle right to the floor and started weaving back and forth in a huge serpentine fashion. With the car full of gas and me full of alcohol, I had gone, no doubt, completely nuts at the wheel.

Halfway out in the middle of this open field I lost control. The car made two complete spins and died, the dust in the air so thick that we had no way of knowing which direction we were facing. My two screaming passengers, very angry at my performance, only brought my madness to a higher level.

Not having a clue of which way I was headed, I quickly restarted the car, spun the wheel all the way to the left, put my foot to the floor and began spinning doughnuts round and around until the car bounced to a halt and died for the second time.

This time Bill reached over and grabbed, the keys from the ignition making it impossible for me to ignite a third round of mobile insanity. Again the dust was so thick it took several minutes for the headlights to pierce through the settling dust, revealing an awesome sight.

As the three of us sat there with our mouths slowly dropping open, we witnessed people all around us, in every direction, getting up with their sleeping bags and blankets in hand. The open field had been full of sleeping people who had come to spend the whole three days at the festival.

Somehow, I had torn through this field pulling an insane, chaotic, stupid stunt without running over a single person! Without one person trying to pull me from the car and beat me senseless, which is what I deserved, they silently vacated the field and disappeared into the surrounding tree line.

More than dust settled in the sobering silence of that moment. I was sick inside knowing that I was as irresponsible as the last few minutes had proven me to be. All sorts of "what could've happened's" started running in my mind and, quite frankly, they still do.

Anyway, we forgot about going to see the festival site that night and with Bill in the driver's seat, made our way back to Callas. I came away from that midnight ride aware, once and for all, that sometimes bad things are just not allowed to happen. It all depends on who has ... the Wheel of Control.

CHAPTER SIX

CHARLIE'S ANGELS

The O'Hare Airport in Chicago was a nightmare to us because of the strict security that always had to be dealt with. If our layover times between flights were any length at all, we would be followed around by plainclothes agents who seemed, by their actions, to be convinced that we were up to some sort of illegal trafficking. If they had been more thorough in checking us, they would have proven to be on track.

However, they were dealing with folks who were used to going from country to country carrying things that were out of bounds. International borders were always a drag, but crossing into Canada from O'Hare kept us on our toes, to say the least.

We were headed into the Canadian leg of our tour at the time and looking forward to working in Leonard Cohen's home-land. It was always strange to me that wherever we toured outside the United States, Leonard was number one in the peoples' eyes and Dylan was number two. However, once back in the USA, Dylan was always number one and no one seemed to even know who Leonard was.

After being stranded for several hours with no flights leaving due to weather, we decided to rent a few cars and drive to Canada in hopes of making our first show on time. That day I endured a long ride I will never forget. Charlie Daniels, our bass player at the time, and I were passengers in a car being driven by Bob Johnston. Bob produced Leonard's albums then and was playing keyboards with us when we toured.

The snow was deep and the roads were barely passable, but the beautiful, snow-covered Canadian countryside softened the edge of making the attempt. We stocked up on plenty of vintage wines, along with French bread and an assortment of cheeses. Charlie and his guitar occupied the entire back seat, with me in the passenger's seat up front. Once we were out on the open road, it started snowing. At first it was only flurries, but soon we could tell that a pretty good storm was building up.

As we rolled on into the late afternoon drinking our wine and enjoying our food (as well as some great smoke that we just happened to have along with us), I started to notice that we were traveling a little faster than what you would call "a safe speed" under these conditions.

Charlie had broken out his guitar and was now into his second hour of singing to us from the back seat. He didn't seem to be concerned about Bob's driving, so I didn't say anything.

What a great backseat concert we enjoyed that day as Charlie dug far back into his oldest bag of original songs. I was then, and still am, convinced that he is at his best with just an acoustic guitar and his songs. Most folks are unaware that he wrote songs, which were recorded by a lot of stars back when he was just a starving, nightclub-playing songwriter. Even Elvis had a hit with one of Charlie's co-written (Joy Bowers) songs entitled, "It Hurts Me." These were the days before The Charlie Daniels Band, and in the back seat of this speeding car was the real Charlie, in my opinion.

I first met Charlie in 1967. Clive Davis and Dick Asher had signed my group West to Epic Records and we had returned to Nashville to record our second album.

At that time, and for many years to follow, when in Nashville I stayed at the Holiday Inn at 1800 West End Avenue right off Music Row. It hasn't been a Holiday Inn for years now, but in the 60s, it was definitely a nice place for Nashville and also close to CBS studios where we recorded.

I knew of Charlie through a friend. I was told he was a great writer and that if I wanted to check him out before agreeing to meet with him, all I had to do was drive out to a club called The Hound's Tooth and there I could see him in action.

I knew of Charlie through a friend. I was told he was a great writer and that if I wanted to check him out before agreeing to meet with him, all I had to do was drive out to a club called The Hound's Tooth and there I could see him in action.

Well, in 1967, I had to think twice about walking in some red neck bar with hair down to my shoulders and wreaking of cannabis, Patuoli oil, and carrying who knows what. In those days I got a haircut when the length of the hair equaled the length of the stair. So, me being in the South in the '60s should have promoted me straight from the airport to the barber chair, and I knew it.

However, after getting to know Charlie, I did end up at this club, which turned out to be just a typical night club and, yes, Charlie kicked ass and took no prisoners when it came to bowling over the packed house.

My first visual of Charlie was one I shall not forget. He knocked on the door of my room #426. We always made reservations far in advance to get #426 and for good reason, it was a corner room on the top floor. The Holiday Inn had outdoor room walks back then and with #426 being on the outside corner, we always had wind blowing by on two sides of the room. This elevated our comfort level about our smoke being detected easily.

But, back to Charlie. There at my door stood a cartoon-like character if ever I saw one. Charlie was as big as a mountain. He stood well over six feet tall, about a hundred pounds overweight, wearing horn rimmed glasses with clothes that may have fit at some point, but not today.

He said, "Hi, I'm Charlie Daniels. Bob sent me," as he stuck out a hand missing one finger. I shook that hand noticing the other holding a guitar. After introducing himself to a couple of my band members who were with me, Charlie said, "I got a story song that you boys need to have on your album."

Well, he didn't look like someone who could musically impress us (we being hot shots from California and all), but given the invitation to show us what he had, Charlie plopped down on the bed, straddled a corner and laid an old gut-string atop a belly to be proud of. He slowly slipped into a thumb pick, unconsciously pushed his thick glasses back up off his nose where they seemed to be intent on staying, and very definitely proceeded to give us all a severe ass whipping along the lines of songwriting.

He stayed for quite a while and in those days it didn't take Charlie two minutes to make a friend. He made friends of each of us that day and, yes, the story song entitled "Shanty Boat" did go on the album.

He enjoyed being with those "San Francisco hippies," and we liked to hang with him. He was with us when we played the Monterey Pop Festival in 1967, and any time we were in Nashville or he in California, we always loved getting together. After West broke up in 1969, Charlie and I worked together on many album projects as session mates.

Unceasingly, Charlie and I played jokes on each other, some cruel and ruthless, but that's just the way it was. In fact, we all played jokes on Charlie, but don't think he wasn't capable of getting even. Believe me, it was an ongoing toss up regarding who was on top at any given time. Running around with us, the only thing that seemed to scare him was getting thrown in jail or hurt and, in my opinion, this car ride had potential in both of these areas, no joke.

The wind was now blowing the snow from bank to bank and across the hood of our car. You couldn't see very far at all in any direction, and directly out front only a car length or two. If I had been driving, we would have been going only 25 or 30 miles per hour. So you can imagine my concern when I looked at the speedometer that was reading over 70!

I was surprised when the faster we went and the more dangerous it became, the more fun Charlie seemed to have. This was a true role reversal for us because, as a rule, he never really jumped in there when it came to some of the hair-raising stunts that I normally got us into.

Back then, the psychedelic existence we lived, with mind-altering substances aboard at all times, you had to be unconcerned about going to jail in order to be comfortable. Charlie was usually apprehensive about most ideas that came into our heads, but I tried to keep in mind that he had a wife and child at home to think about. This day he wasn't apprehensive about anything and I sure enjoyed him being with us on that ride.

For over two hours we flew along at speeds that were undeniably suicidal. The car was always sideways or just about to go sideways. Every time I yelled at Bob to "slow this damn thing down," Charlie would roar laughing and call me some kind of a punk-ass name. It was like he knew we weren't going to crash and was taking advantage of getting even with me for a lot of the teasing I'd given him in the past.

Now, I've always been pretty strong behind the wheel of a car, but Bob certainly gave me one hell of a driving lesson that day. Somewhere along the way I finally reserved myself to the fact that if we hadn't wrecked the car by now, then maybe we weren't going to. I swallowed my fear, along with my good sense, and tried to have a good time.

I know that someone was watching over us because there is just no other reason for us not to have been taken out of this world. I realized later that with Charlie being so out of character that day, he knew, maybe unconsciously, something that I did not. He knew that we were safe from harm and protected by ... Charlie's Angels.

CHAPTER SEVEN

JEREMY

After years of playing shows the world over, it's easy to look back and speak to the ones which stand out for reasons unto themselves. As you might expect, often the ones you thought would be just another concert turn out to be the standouts.

Occasionally a city gets booked that you immediately know will be unforgettable. This is the feeling I had when I learned of our group being scheduled to play in Berlin at the same hall where Adolf Hitler gave one of his last bone-chilling deliveries to the German people just prior to the end of World War II. This story begins in London just a day or so before our departure.

A young Englishman named Bob Potter was making quite a name for himself at the time as a recording engineer. His credits included names such as Joe Cocker, The Grease Band, Average White Band, Leon Russell, Mad Dogs and Englishmen, and others. Columbia Records had hired him to tour with us to record our concerts with Leonard Cohen as chief engineer in charge.

He was thin, smartly dressed and very intelligent. In fact, he was a little too smart for his age, in my opinion. His IQ was way up there and he was one of those people you hear about getting through college by the age of sixteen. He was very creative and had attended some art school in England where he met up with Peter Townsend and "mates" of The Who, who were enrolled to study art long before they formed as a band. He bordered on being schizophrenic and at times displayed an uncontrollable temper.

I've witnessed him throwing a wine bottle through the plate glass window of a recording studio control room just because some piece of gear wasn't performing properly. He also was very compassionate and would stand up for what he knew to be right. This is the side of Potter that manifested itself on this day, our day of departure from London to Berlin.

I had been staying at Potter's house for a few days prior to leaving for Berlin, which would be the first concert date of a European tour. We had been working at Island Studios in London. I was doing some guitar overdubs on a Hoyt Axton album and Potter was the recording engineer.

I always enjoyed being around Hoyt. He, like Charlie Daniels, always impressed me more when he presented his songs with just an acoustic guitar. Prior to recording some of this album I spent a couple of weeks in a wonderful home located in Tunbridge Wells, England.

Hoyt came out and stayed a day or so to work with me on his music. The home was constructed from the remains of an old

Spanish galleon that was several hundred years old. The owner was Tony Stratton-Smith who, at the time, owned a record label in London. I spent a lot of time there during one summer and it was there one late, late night that Hoyt first played for us things like "Boney Fingers," "Mary Makes Magic" and several others of which I had the pleasure of contributing my guitar work to.

I can't explain how surprised, when walking into an English pub, the people were to actually see a man of his physical size. The average Englishman would react as if Sasquatch had just walked in. Being with Hoyt in England was like walking around with Hoss Cartwright (of *Bonanza*) in Munchkinland.

This particular summer was a rather painful time for him. He was going through a divorce and was in the process of losing a home that he had built himself. He described his house in detail to me and I would have loved to have seen it personally. Everything was built to his size and I'm sure that it was a great place.

Once finished with the work to be done on Hoyt's album, Potter and I moved on to an album by Michael Martin Murphey. This album had been recorded in Nashville and was entitled "Geronimo's Cadillac." It was complete except for a few songs that had to be mixed.

I remember the last song, entitled "The Lights Of The City," being a problem to us. The producer told us he was finished with the album and to ship it to the States to be manufactured. The song featured an organ part that very obviously had wrong chords in one section. Our pointing this out to the producer did no good. He had been wanting to get back to

Island was owned by Chris Blackwell. It was a great studio and was built in the basement of a very old church.

Nashville for several weeks now and quite frankly, didn't give a damn about wrong chords on some new kid's album.

Potter and I kept dealing with the fact that this was just plain wrong and, though we had never met Michael M., we couldn't feel right about letting product go out like this on anyone. A few nights later in the wee hours, and after consuming quite a lot of cognac, the problem finally got the best of us. We hired a car and drove back to Island Studios where we had been working.

Island was owned by Chris Blackwell. It was a great studio and was built in the basement of a very old church. I had been told many stories about this place and how it was haunted. The part we occupied was once a crypt. Several people had seen what they reported to be the ghost of Jimi Hendrix.

The story goes that a young black man who was not a stranger would come by from time to time. This young man did not play guitar but on occasion would go out into the grand room of the studio, turn his back to the booth, strap on a guitar and commence to fire down licks that only Hendrix himself, could have played. I never put much stock into the story but, after hearing it, sometimes being there late at night was a little scary.

Anyway, once we arrived and made our way to the control room, we took a razor blade and cut the final mix of "The Lights Of The City" from the master reel and watched it fall to the floor.

Pulling out the multi-track, we spent the next several hours remixing the song, burying the bad chords on the organ track. We then spliced our mix of the song onto the master reel going to the States and, to my knowledge, neither the producer nor Michael ever knew of our late night, vigilante endeavor.

After spending the following day trying to rest at Potter's home, we crashed rather early and arose the next morning. This was the day of departure on our trek to Berlin. Since our plane was not scheduled to leave until late morning, we enjoyed brown eggs and soldiers (soft boiled, brown eggs along with strips of toast used for dunking, after breaking a hole in the top by smacking it with a spoon) with fresh orange juice spiked with champagne.

With this meal, Potter was scanning the morning paper when I noticed the monster in him start to appear. His face became beet red as he rifled through the article that told of a child molester named Jeremy who, after several months of investigation, had become the primary suspect in the case. This person had come from the same area where Potter grew up and the charge came as no surprise.

It was not the first time this man had been accused of this sort of crime. Potter became enraged and started kicking furniture, throwing things around the room, and swearing that he would blow this pervert away if he could get to him. I tried to calm him down, but having dealt with his temper on prior occasions, I knew this would be no easy task.

Soon it was time to head for the airport, which took his mind off Jeremy for the time being. Once at the airport, our tour manager Donovan stashed us in the lounge and went about his usual duties of securing boarding passes for everyone and dealing with the checking procedures of instruments and baggage.

Potter was still bringing up Jeremy, which made me wonder if he himself had been abused as a child. He just couldn't, or wouldn't, let go of the subject. I thought for a while that I might talk him through it by agreeing with him about everything. Each time he came up with a different way of how people like this Jeremy guy should be tortured, I would say, "You're right." Well, this came back to bite me once we arrived in Berlin. On our flight to Berlin, I sat away from him because I was tired of hearing him go on and on about Jeremy.

I had just made it through immigration when I noticed Donovan and some of the crew scuffling with someone out in the main terminal. When I got to them, it was Potter being held by two of the crew with Donovan right up in his face yelling, "Stop this shit before you got us all arrested!"

To everyone's surprise, after listening to Potter rave all day about this child abusing bastard from his home neighborhood, and as luck would have it, there, not 50 feet away was Jeremy. In flesh and blood, right there coming through customs, Jeremy seemed not to have a care in the world. Joking with security and laughing aloud, he was noticed by all.

Potter would have definitely tried to kill him if Donovan and crew had not contained him. Donovan made him aware that if he were to be arrested it would not only be bad for him, but it would look bad for all of us and reflect directly back to Leonard. CBS wouldn't tolerate him being out of control and landing in jail and they would simply replace him with another engineer. Potter had so looked forward to going on this tour that I think the thought of missing out helped calm him down.

Soon we were in the limos and headed for the hotel. As usual, the hotel we checked into was one of the most elegant in town. I knew this night was a night off, with our concert being scheduled for the following evening. Berlin felt scary. This was long before the wall came down and there were plenty of beer halls and such where an American could easily get into deep trouble. I once barely escaped with my life while frequenting beer halls in Germany with Anne Drews. I knew that this night, since it was our first one out, could prove to be a long one.

Once checked into my room I lay down to rest, intending on hooking up with everyone later. Around six o'clock that evening I went down to the lobby of this magnificent old hotel. I had one cognac in the lounge and ordered another, along with a very thin cigar that came three to a tin. I never remembered the name of those cigars and have not run into them since, but with cognac, they were wonderful.

I then sat down in a huge overstuffed chair that faced the elevator, allowing me to see anyone traveling in our bunch who might come down. I hadn't been there long when the elevator doors opened. The person who stepped out almost made me swallow the cigar, and did make me fire that glass of cognac straight down. Yea, you guessed it, that damn Jeremy was in the same hotel as us. I couldn't believe my eyes ... this was just what we did not need.

There was no way we could stay the three days we were scheduled to be there without Potter causing big problems. Surely he would, at some point, run into Jeremy and when he did, all hell would break loose. Luckily, Jeremy walked straight from the elevator to the front door, stepped into a waiting car and was gone.

Immediately I returned to my room, called Donovan and summoned him to meet me in the lounge, post haste. About 15 minutes later I proceeded to the lounge, figuring I'd given him enough time to get ready, and walked in noticing him sitting alone at the bar. He had already secured a cognac for both of us and as I approached, he handed one to me and motioned to a table in the far corner of the room. Other than the bartender we were the only ones in this dimly lit, but beautiful, extension of the magnificent hotel lobby.

The location of this table would allow us to go unnoticed by any of our troop who might walk by. I told Donovan that Jeremy was checked in to this hotel. He couldn't believe that we had drawn such an unlucky card. After the ordeal at the airport, we knew something would inevitably come out of this that we may not be able to control.

I began to think of the possibility of arranging something that would allow Potter to have a go at Jeremy at some point during our stay, but in a nonviolent way. Something that would give Potter almost as much pleasure as strangling this asshole but without laying a finger on him. This would be a hard one to come up with, but anything's possible. Doing something like this, which would have to be great, would provide the chance for us to get through the next few days and on to our next gig, leaving the Potter/Jeremy problem behind. I began to look upon this as an amusing challenge and with that, my wheels started turning. We left the lounge a short while later with plenty of food for thought.

By now it was mid-evening and a few of us hit the streets to check out this city of ominous feelings. As we walked past huge city buildings, we could see bullet holes from back in the days of Nazi Germany that were still in disrepair. These visual scars from an unforgotten piece of history were purposely left unattended, and for that very reason, to never forget.

Not long after leaving the hotel we grabbed a taxi and directed the driver to take us to the main gate at the Berlin Wall. There we encountered two very tall towers manned with armed German soldiers who could easily be seen from all directions. The intensity of being there this cold, dark night, left a frozen image that stays unto itself in my mind. I realized that the pictures we've all seen regarding World War II must have influenced my initial reactions to the atmosphere around me.

But, I was also aware of a foreboding presence in the air that was very real. I was told you could walk along the wall on either side of the huge gate without alarming anyone. However, should you make the mistake of touching the wall for any reason you could and, if seen by a guard, would be shot.

Having played many concerts in other cities in Germany, I had long before this night made up my mind that the general reaction to long-haired musicians from America, socially, was poor. People were not very friendly out in the streets and I had problems at times staying positive. It bothered me to see someone feel the softness of a flower with the back of their hand, or refer to hail as "ice bombs." Things like that added to the insensitivity that seemed to be ever present.

But just as a statement like this
comes out of my
mouth, I'm reminded
that one of the real
true loves of my
life, Anne Drews
(another story) was German
and I'd given much thought of spending the rest of my life right there in Germany with her—go figure!!

The overall feelings I lived with each time we toured Germany always made me apprehensive when taking the stage with Leonard Cohen. You never knew what he might do or say that could cause things to get very weird.

There was the time in Hamburg that qualifies of due mention. We had completed the first half of the show, taken a 30-minute intermission, and were three or four songs into the second half of the concert. It always seemed to be this part of the evening that he would pull something. I'm not saying that he'd plan some stunt, he was a very spontaneous person, but as an evening unfolded he would get a little loose at times and come up with crazy ideas.

This time he decided to tell the audience that he was about to make a gesture that had "stood for evil and now, here tonight for just one moment in time, let it stand for peace and love." With that, he threw his stiffened right arm up and out into the air and clicked his heels together.

This possibly could have accomplished whatever was in his scrambled brain at the time had it not been for one thing— they didn't understand English. The place went nuts. People came out of their chairs and had to be restrained by security from coming right up on stage after us.

One guard actually wrestled a man to the floor right at our feet. The man had produced a gun and was trying to get close enough to us to use it. Finally, after quite a length of chaos, we did play a few more songs but, needless to say, whatever magic we had cultivated that evening was gone.

Well, I could go on and on retrieving incidents of spontaneous craziness provided by Leonard Cohen, from invitations to participate in red wine enemas to performing the encore of a wonderful concert while standing on his head.

But now, this night in Berlin was not for me to think about being, or not being, apprehensive about the upcoming concert. Also, I was not going to waste time on past incidents that fuel such apprehensions. My thought patterns for tonight would be directed toward finding an approach to the Jeremy/Potter problem.

As I said earlier, it would be great to come up with something that would, in some way, get to Jeremy in a very strong way without actually allowing Porter to physically attack him. From the outside, it seems rather ridiculous to be involved in such a thing while in the midst of a concert tour, or for that matter, any time. However, I must admit I did get enjoyment out of dealing with it.

I knew the possibility of Jeremy checking out of our hotel the very next day was there. Today's occurrences, from the newspaper at breakfast to the odds of him arriving at the airport simulta- neously with us, along with him staying at the exact hotel we were in, left me thinking hard about it.

The plan slowly started to come together over the course of the evening. I decided on scaring Jeremy, if I could, in a way that Alfred Hitchcock might play with the unknown as he did on so many outings. The unknown I had to work with was that Jeremy didn't see the ruckus Potter had created at the airport. He had no idea anyone near him even knew who he was. This gave me room to move in.

With a 22-man film crew traveling with us filming a movie of the tour, later to be titled *Bird On A Wire*, I had plenty of bodies to help execute whatever I came up with. I chose nine, counting Donovan and Potter, to take part in a very simple and hopefully effective course of action.

Back at the hotel in Donovan's room, I explained the maneuver in detail to all of them. We ended the evening around 2:00 AM with a promise by all to meet me in the lobby at 8:00 AM sharp the next morning.

When morning came I made sure to be down in the lobby on time. Each member of my little posse was present and accounted for. I had one of the film crew guys bring a car around and park in front of the hotel in case we needed to leave by car. You see, I had no way of knowing whether or not we would be on foot.

I positioned each of my people around the lobby in separate spots. I grabbed a cup of coffee and sat down in yesterday's familiar over-stuffed chair facing the elevator. We would now remain at our posts until Jeremy came out of that elevator.

After more than an hour and just at the moment I was about to lose some of my squad due to impatience, the elevator opened and out walked Jeremy.

As planned, no one moved until I did. Jeremy passed in front of me and continued across the lobby toward the front door. I eased out of my chair and fell in behind him a few yards back. At that point Donovan fell in behind me maintaining the

With a 22-man film crew traveling with us filming a movie of the tour, later to be titled *Bird On A Wire*, I had plenty of bodies to help execute whatever I came up with.

same few yards distance, followed by Potter, and the others followed suit. We were all ready to pile into our waiting car, if needed, but that became unnecessary as Jeremy exited left out of the hotel and proceeded to leave on foot.

What a visual. Here we have a guy who has flown to a foreign country, spent one night in a hotel, and is now being followed down the street by a long line of people, all from other countries, who know exactly who he is and he's totally unaware that anything is going on.

There was good reason for our following Jeremy in a line separated from one another. This would come into play once we found out where he was going. After leaving the hotel he walked to the corner of the block, crossed the street and proceeded half way down the next block. At this point he stopped and entered a bank. Seconds later I arrived and looked in through the large glass doors in order to keep visual contact with him.

As I peered inside I could see Jeremy taking his place in one of six or eight long lines of people waiting for their turn at a teller's window. I couldn't help but notice the magnitude of the bank itself. It was like one of the old Bank of America banks in the USA, with 50-foot ceilings, pillars, and marbled everything—it was huge and absolutely gorgeous.

By now, Donovan had caught up with me. I turned him back and together we quickly met Potter and the others who were approaching one by one. We figured the odds of Jeremy returning to the hotel, once he had completed his bank transaction, were pretty good. With this in mind and with everyone

114

well versed on the plan, they all positioned themselves in various places between the bank and the hotel. Donovan and I returned to and entered the bank, leaving Potter outside. His position would be two or three doors down toward the hotel.

As we entered the bank, we could see Jeremy in one of the center customer lines. I motioned to Donovan, telling him to secure a place in one of the far lines. I took a place in the first line, which was near the front door. Now, as you can visualize, we have Jeremy in one of the center lines now halfway up to the teller while two complete strangers flank him on both sides to his rear. We waited for a minute or so and then put the plan in motion.

In a very loud but whispery voice, I blurted out, "JEREMY!"

Jeremy immediately looked around to see who in that bank could be addressing him. I kept my eyes straight ahead as though I had said nothing. Soon, from the other side of the bank, Donovan spoke out the same, "JEREMY!"

This, coming from another direction, took Jeremy totally by surprise. As I had a few moments earlier, Donovan acted as though he'd said nothing. This made Jeremy extremely uncomfortable.

After a few more minutes passed, and once again in a loud scratchy whisper, I called, "JEREMY" once more.

Donovan followed suit a minute or so later. This time Jeremy freaked. He couldn't figure out where or who was calling his name.

He was so frightfully disturbed and confused, I could see his next progression would be full-blown panic. This time I waited a little longer to throw out the spark which would ignite a helter-skelter display by Jeremy and accelerate the plan to a rapid-paced frenzy.

When he was one person away from the teller, I shouted in full voice, "JER-R-R-R-REMY!"

Well, this time Jeremy didn't show any concern for where or his name had come. He bolted from the line and hit the front door of that bank like a turpentined cat. As anticipated, he headed straight back toward the hotel.

Little did he know, Potter was standing at his post just two doors down. As he frantically scurried by Potter, he was once again confronted with, "JER-R-R-R-REMY."

This stopped him dead in his tracks. He saw Potter leaning in a doorway and as their eyes locked in on each other, again Potter said, "JER-R-R-R-REMY. Come here Jeremy."

Scared out of his wits, Jeremy took off in a flat out run toward the hotel. He had no way of knowing there were six more people to get through along the way who also had but one word for him, "JER-R-R-R-REMY!" - "JER-R-R-R-REMY!" - "JER-R-R-R-REMY!"

Hysteria look over before Jeremy reached the hotel. He ran out into the busy boulevard and was almost taken down as cars swerved and skidded to keep from hitting him. Potter said that in the brief moments on the sidewalk while face to face, he noticed that Jeremy had "lost his salt." I later learned what Potter meant—he had pissed himself.

Jeremy's mind couldn't begin to put together anything that would come near rationalizing this Twilight Zone-type experience he was caught up in. Somehow, every stranger on the street knew him by name even though he was far away from home. How could he begin to understand? Did this really happen? Did his imagination just get completely out of control?

Well. I'm here to let you know that this did really happen and it did do to Jeremy exactly what we wanted it to. We never saw him after that morning and except for a couple of drinks toasting a serious conformation of a job well done, the lot of us never boasted about this episode to any length.

Potter let it go as well. We continued our concert tour, and I never knew what became of JER-R-R-R-REMY!

CHAPTER EIGHT

CASH IN - CASH OUT

It was cold in Nashville—January 1969, almost as cold as London in January—but not quite.

I know about January cold in London from experience. I played a three-week stint at a club in London named Ronnie Scott's one January.

London England has its own kind of cold. It matters not what kind of coat or overcoat you wear. The freezing wind comes right through, chilling you to the bone. I don't think I ever got warm the whole time on that trip.

Anyway, January 1969 in Nashville was cold, cold.

After spending the holidays at home in the San Francisco bay area, it was great starting out 1969 with several projects ahead. I was in Nashville to play guitar on a couple of albums that Bob Johnston was producing, of which he was kind enough to include me in on the sessions.

This time we were only able to get in one session per day at 10:00 AM in Columbia Studio A. The afternoons and evenings were taken up by the whole Johnny Cash TV Show crew, recording and rehearsing things connected with the show that was to, and did, begin airing the following June.

On a daily basis, when our 10:00 session ended at 1:00 PM, Johnston and I would be out of the studio and quickly gone. Once in the car, it was get totally loaded and chase down the rest of the day—"Free-Flight."

This day, at the end of our session, I noticed Johnston in the control room having some sort of meeting with Cash and a different bunch of people than were usually there. Later on that day he shared with me who those people were, and what their meeting was about.

The people were from Los Angeles and were meeting with Cash and Johnston about a movie they were in the process of filming.

The movie would be entitled: *I Walk The Line* staring Gregory Peck and Tuesday Weld and about a small town sheriff (Peck) falling in love with a beautiful young thing (Weld) who is less than half his age. The storyline would revolve around this taboo love affair and be supported musically with all Johnny Cash songs.

There was an extra perk that came out of their meeting. Turned out, they had a spot in the movie that they still needed two songs for. Johnston told me that if we could come up with two original songs right away, we could track them on our 10:00 AM session the

120

following day and get Cash to pilot the vocals when they all got there at 1:00 PM.

Johnston's theory was that if they watched Cash sing them, the songs would have an excellent chance of actually making it into the film.

That night at Johnston's house, he said each song really only needed to be about a minute long to fill the time slot for this specific scene in the film. For some time I had been foolin' around with a couple of ideas—country oriented—that Johnston felt would be great as choruses to work from in writing the needed songs.

Once he had my choruses in his mind, and right there at his old upright piano in his den, he effortlessly came up with a verse for each song. Since all they needed was about one minute in each spot, a verse and a chorus on each song could work-if they liked what we had.

Johnston said, "Listen man, if Cash likes these enough to pilot the vocal tomorrow, and the L.A. folks watch him at that damn mic singin' em, we're in!"

The next day during our 10:00 AM session, we took a few minutes and tracked the two songs, just one verse and one chorus on each. At Johnston's request, Cash showed up 30 minutes early. We showed him what we had.

Cash said, with that smile that always seemed to come from one side of his mouth, the tracks would easily work in the two short scenes. But, he added, "Who knows what the L.A. folks will think."

By now, the L.A. people had arrived and when they were all comfortable in the control room, Johnston pulled the trigger. Well, exactly like Johnston predicted, when bigger-than-life Cash stepped to the mic and fired off the two partial song "pilots," the folks from L.A. were so in awe—there was no doubt—the songs were definitely in the movie *I Walk The Line* (released 1970).

During the previous few years, before all of this, I had met John and been around him on several occasions at Columbia Studios there in Nashville. He always had time to talk, looked ya right in the eye, and ya had no "Big Time Ego" to deal with.

Throughout the years there has always been an "anything goes" rule between me, Bob Johnston, and Bill Donovan (the American and European tour manager for Leonard Cohen) when it comes to gotcha practical jokes on each other. So, nearing my birthday (Feb. 15, 1969) on a crisp California morning and down on the water at my home on the bay, I received a phone call from Bob Johnston. I thought it was a joke when he said he wanted me to come and be part of the Johnny Cash *Live At San Quentin* album, scheduled to be recorded at the prison around the end of the month.

I knew he didn't need me to play guitar as John always performed with his own band, The Tennessee Three. I said: "Bob, San Quentin is a maximum security prison—they won't let me in there. Whata-ya-think, they're gonna let ya have a guest list?"

Bob simply replied, "Fuck'em—You're part of the 'Production Team.' I'm Producing this damn thing. What are they gonna say? If I say you're part of the team, that'll be the end of it, trust me."

As it turned out, he was not joking, I did go in as part of the team that 24th day of February 1969, and knowing it would become a bit of true music history, I was then, and have always been, very appreciative of Bob for including me in on that special day.

Traveling south along the east side of the San Francisco bay from my home in Crockett, about half way to San Francisco, you pass through Richmond. From Richmond's viewpoint, straight across the bay is San Rafael. At the water's edge of San Rafael, and very visible, looms San Quentin Prison. A scary visual in every respect, San Quentin houses the badest of the bad, from its Death Row to its laundry room. I know because, you see, I grew up in Richmond.

To explain growing up in Richmond would be like explaining growing up at the North Pole to someone who was raised in Florida, if talkin' about the climate, but I'm not. Per capita, Richmond has a higher crime rate (especially shootings) than Oakland, California, which was one of the highest in the country.

Like a comedian said: "It's a place where ya can get shot—while you're gettin' shot." The gangs were out of control, the cops were afraid of them, and even stopping at a 7-Eleven after dark was taking a chance every time out. Now, I must admit, my pre-teen and teenage years were not as bad as they would be today in Richmond. But, even back then, if you compared Richmond with its surrounding cities, Richmond was far worse.

Walking into San Quentin with all the Nashville Columbia Records bunch made me apprehensive right from the start.

During my later teens and early 20s, my dad would occasionally say: "Be careful out there. Fallin' in with the wrong crowd or you'll be walking around out there in the middle of the Bay on Alcatraz or locked up in San Quentin for who knows how long."

Quite a few people I knew proved him to be absolutely right, because that was exactly what happened to them. Looking back, I can honestly say that from age 16-26, I was standing in some club with a guitar in my hands while they were out there getting into trouble. The love of music and playing guitar, I think, helped me to not (as my dad said) fall too closely in with the wrong crowd.

A few of these old "cronies" of mine that did their time in prison were really closer to me than just acquaintances, close enough that I had been inside the walls of San Quentin several times before the day of the Johnny Cash prison show. Visitor's Day at San Quentin was Sunday afternoons and I quiver when I think of the chances we took smuggling things in there. Had we been caught, we would have been in deep trouble ourselves.

Through the 60s, drugs were a "staple" in our lives. Having drugs, as a prisoner, was like them having money. You could

124

trade drugs for almost anything you needed on the inside, and using on the inside, no doubt, makes the time easier to do.

To graphically explain how we accomplished our Visitor's Day goals would be a bit unsettling and therefore, I think, unnecessary. The reason for bringing all of this up is to point out that walking into San Quentin with all the Nashville Columbia Records bunch made me apprehensive right from the start. I guess the feeling was, sort of, like someone leading a double life. I didn't want some of the Nashville folks to know I had friends who were inmates, and at the same time, these guys on the inside were close enough to me to take the chances I just spoke to— crazy, I know! Even though it was somewhat troubling, I knew I'd just have to let it play out.

Who knows, maybe I would get through the day without seeing any of my "Richmond Buds"—or if I did, maybe they'd have the good sense to keep their mouths shut, right? Dream on.

The morning of Feb. 24, 1969 (San Quentin Day), by around 8:30 or 9:00 AM, I was out the door of my little cottage on the bay and on my way to pick up Johnston in Marin County. We rolled up to the front gates of San Quentin about 11:00 AM.

The guard in the gate booth instructed us to closely follow a Prison guard driving a small vehicle (a little golf cart pick-up type) to where we could park near the large cafeteria where the show was set to take place. Risers had been brought in to create a stage at one end and when we arrived everything was pretty well set up and ready to go.

Johnston immediately summoned the chief engineer. He made sure everything was closely mic'd to ensure the music tracks, getting from the stage to the mobile recording truck outside, were clean and sterile. He then instructed them to set up mikes around the entire stage area to feed a separate and constantly running 2 TRK recorder—a practice that Johnston was famous for. The separate 2 TRK not only captures the total "ambiance" in the room (great for adding warmth when mixing the album), but also anything and everything that anyone might say.

Some might call this recording overkill and expensive to do, but Bob was known for never missing a single moment when magic was goin' down. He said, "Cash and a bunch of prisoners all in one room? Ya better be ready for anything."

With that in mind, and in my opinion, a few exchanges did occur between John and the prisoners that would have been great on the album, but for one reason or another were dropped. I would imagine that John himself excluded them during the editing and mixing process, because Johnston would have left them in— he always loved that stuff, as did I.

Behind the stage a curtain went right up to the ceiling, creating a narrow backstage area. A very tall, gaunt looking man was standing about a third of the way in from stage-right and I recognized him immediately as being Ralph Gleason. Ralph was one of the two leading music critics in the bay area. For many, many years he wrote for *The San Francisco Chronicle*. I knew him prior to this day because he had written reviews on the West albums (Epic Records), the group of which I was a member.

For a reason unknown to me at the time, he was very, very agitated. In fact, he was acting like he was full-blown frightened. He was pacing back and forth, taking off his trenchcoat, putting the coat back on, starting to speak to someone and turning away from them before speaking—flat-out upset. He gave the impression that he might just walk out and leave before the show even started.

About 20 feet to his right was a table with coffee and snacks. Two of the engineers were there at the table and I could see them also watching Ralph and they were, sort of, inconspicuously laughing. I walked over and asked them if they knew why Ralph was so freaked out. I was not really surprised with their answer.

It seems that a while earlier, Bob Johnston had told Ralph that the prison held about 3,500 prisoners and the room we were in only held 700. Therefore, the warden decided that only the most well-behaved inmates would be allowed to attend the show. This meant that over 2,000 of the real bad-asses were not allowed and they were coming unglued! He told Ralph that they were setting their bedding on fire and throwing it out the windows and the possibility of a full-on prison riot was brewing in the buildings all around us.

"You boys need to be careful here."
—Johnny Cash

It was one of those "ya had to be there" scenes but, that day, Ralph Gleason was actually convinced by Johnston that our lives were in danger and that if the situation kept escalating, people could end up dead. I wasn't around when Ralph was told the truth, that he had been taken in by believing this cooked up yarn, spun by Bob, but I did wonder later if, in any way, it affected his review of the show.

You might say that these kinds of antics played on "music critics" could prove harmful later on but, as I said, the practical joking was ongoing and watching Ralph squirm certainly qualified as high ranking on the scale of giggles.

We were still 40 minutes to an hour ahead of show-time when I noticed Johnston over by one of the side-stage exits. He was accompanied by a short guy whom I immediately recognized. The guy with him was Jann Wenner, founder of *Rolling Stone* magazine, evidentially there to cover the show personally.

The exit they were at led out into the prison yard which we had been allowed to use as a parking area. Bob motioned for me to come with them, so I started making my way through the narrow, crowded back-stage area toward them. Almost to the door, a strong hand firmly took hold of my right shoulder from behind. As I started to turn, Cash's head was close to my ear and in that low, unmistakable Hello-I'm-Johnny-Cash voice, said, "You boys need to be careful here."

His slight concern was obvious and pointing to the fact that it's one thing to pull a joke on someone like Ralph Gleason, a local bay area music critic, and yet another to piss off someone like Jann Wenner who reaches music fans on a global level with every article he writes. He knew Johnston was on one of his rolls and could easily see this one coming.

As I glanced back and up at him, I laughingly said, "John; I really don't even want to go out there, but I know what ya mean."

Once outside, Johnston told me that he'd agreed to give Jann an interview for *Rolling Stone* and they were going to go sit in our car to get away from all the noise. He said, "It won't take long, come on and sit with us."

As we approached the car, which as only about a 100 feet away, Bob asked Jann to give him the note pad he was carrying. He told Jann that to avoid being misquoted, as had happened to him many times in the past, he wanted to do this one a little different.

Putting Jann and me in the front sea, Bob sprawled out in the back seat with the notepad. He had decided to actually write down, word for word, each question that would be asked by Jann and then write down, word for word, each answer.

You could see that Jann wasn't very excited about this way of going about an interview, but he went along with it anyway. This interview may have been important to Jann because of the fact that, at this very point in time, Bob was producing many of the biggest names in music other than Cash and was rather hard to pin down for an interview by anyone.

So, for the next 30 or so minutes, Jann would ask a question and Bob would write it down. He didn't answer the questions aloud, but would sit there silently writing down the answers for Jann to read later. Once Bob finished writing an answer, he would say, "Next question."

When the interview was over, and Bob noticing that it was definitely time for him to be back inside, he tossed the notepad into the front seat with me and Jann and was gone in a flash.

Well, as I said earlier, Johnston's practical joke bone was glowing that day and he was "on a roll." When we opened the pad, and as you've probably guessed by now, yes, it was totally BLANK!

The show started with just John and "The Tennessee Three" and added, as it moved along, the entire Cash family offering. June and John did their duets, the Carter background thing was great and even Carl Perkins added a touch of class as he played.

There was an obvious difference in the look on John's face, if comparing it to him being in front of a crowd at a normal Johnny Cash concert. That ongoing "caged animal, skin crawling" aura that we were all accustomed to was not present. His genuine smile throughout the show was as if he were just singin' a bunch of songs at a family get-together. He seemed overwhelmingly comfort-able to be there and the inmates were glued to his every move.

Those men knew that that big old street-talkin' Man In Black had somehow found light and had turned his life around. Some had hope in their eyes that said, "If he could do it, so can I."

Everyone in the room could see the inmates lookin' at John and in some way seein' themselves. Also in the room, and from Nashville, were the ones who could see Cash lookin' at the prisoners and seein' Cash.

ABOUT THE AUTHOR

As a teenage guitarist in California, Ron Cornelius cut his musical teeth while backing a list of artists that reads like a "Who's Who" from the 1950s and 1960s. Chubby Checker, Martha and the Vandellas, Smoky Robinson & and the Miracles, Jan & Dean, and Bobby Rydell were among those that young Cornelius shared a stage with, in addition to many other major artists, such as Glen Campbell, Sonny & Cher, Jackie Wilson, The Sherrells, Gene Chandler, and Mary Wells, as they toured his home state.

At age 16, Ron had a major record deal with his own group "The Untouchables" on Dot Records, a major label at the time.

After years as a backing guitarist, Cornelius formed the group, West, which would bring his first national recognition. West appeared in numerous national showcases across the country that resulted in bids from eight major record labels.

In 1967, they signed with Epic Records and appeared in Las Vegas at the CBS Convention. Two albums were cut in Nashville for the label. A single, "Just Like Tom Thumb's Blues" (a Bob Dylan composition), climbed to #17 on the national charts. The group went on to record a third and final LP for Paramount Records before dissolving. Altogether, Ron

Cornelius has had five major record deals as an artist; others included A&M Records and Polydor Records.

In 1969, Ron found himself with Johnny Cash in San Quentin as part of the production team for Cash's album *Live at San Quentin*. Soon after, Ron returned to backing other acts as a lead guitarist, but this time on a remarkable chain of hit albums with some of the biggest names in country and popular music, such as Johnny Cash, Marty Robbins, Lester Flatt & Earl Scruggs, Hoyt Axton, Loudon Wainwright III, and many others. Most notably, Cornelius supplied lead guitar work on seven multi-platinum albums for the legendary Bob Dylan.

Also during this time, Ron helped assemble a band for world renowned singer/songwriter Leonard Cohen, serving as band leader for six major world tours, four albums, and one movie (for which Cornelius won rave reviews for his guitar stylings). The albums were among Cohen's best; *Songs From a Room*, *Leonard Cohen Live*, *Songs of Love and Hate*, and his *Greatest Hits* album (all certified platinum).

The movie, *Bird On A Wire*, produced during his tenure with Cohen, was filmed during a tour that started on St. Patrick's Day in Ireland and ended four months later in Israel. While there, Cornelius composed a song, "Jerusalem," which was recorded by leading Israeli artist Esther Ofarim, with the London Philharmonic Orchestra. "Jerusalem" was also featured on her live album in concert with the Tel Aviv Philharmonic.

Ron also provided his guitar expertise on several motion picture soundtracks. Among them were the films *I Walk the Line* starring Gregory Peck and Tuesday Wells (Ron also composed two songs featured in this movie), *Concrete Cowboy* starring Jerry Reed, *Little Fauss and Big Halsy* starring Robert

Redford and Michael J. Pollard, and *The Big Lebowsky* starring Jeff Bridges and John Goodman.

Ron's next move was to Nashville where, in 1980, he pursued a career as a producer, songwriter, and publisher in addition to his work as a major guitarist. Joining forces with another industry legend, Pete Drake, he served as Professional Manager and Producer of Drake Music Group's Nashville publishing administration service, and later rose to take charge of and produce for The A.T.V. Music Corporation's Nashville office.

At that time, A.T.V. was the 4th largest publisher in the world administering the works of John Lennon and Paul McCartney, as well as a 6,000 song catalog of country music greats!

In 1986, Cornelius founded The Cornelius Companies, an independent Nashville based Production and Publishing entity. Cornelius has represented and administered catalogs for Cabin Fever Entertainment, Inc., Charlie Daniels/Miss Hazel Music, and The Lowery Music Group out of Atlanta, Georgia. Artists such as Faith Hill, Confederate Railroad, David Allen Coe, Alabama, and many more have recorded Songs from the Cornelius catalog.

In 1995, Ron created a record label and Production Company called Gateway Entertainment, Inc., a division of the Cornelius Companies.

Initially directed at the increasingly popular Positive Country radio format, that year Ron's Gateway label racked up an impressive collection of his songs: Eleven top 10s, Eight top 5s, Six #2s, and Two #1 singles, all produced by Ron Cornelius.

Cashbox Magazine honored gateway Entertainment with the Top Label Award in the 1995-year end rank and figures. In 1996, 1997, and 1998, with the competition being Warner-Alliance Records, Reunion Records, Word Records, Homeland Records, and The Brentwood Group, Gateway Entertainment acquired more #1 and top 5 singles than any other label in the Positive Country radio format. Gateway Entertainment received the nationwide radio "Positive Country Label of the Year" award and production credits for 1996 through 1998.

Recent years have witnessed major label recording contracts for acts that Ron has signed, developed, and produced, such as Miko Marks' recent releases. Miko is the first African-American female country artist to win bonafide achievement awards in the history of country music (New Music Weekly's Female Country Vocalist of the Year for 2006).

The Cornelius Companies and Gateway Entertainment, Inc. continue their success because of Ron's knowledge and vast experience in the industry, as well as a lot of hard work and integrity.

In 2015, the one and only Nashville Hall of Fame added another stand-alone exhibit, this time showcasing Ron and his "Country Gentleman" Grestch guitar.

AFTERWORD

"*In Life,* my longest journey has been *from No to Yes.*"
—John Dean Cornelius

(My cousin, who is just four months older than me, not only has the same middle name and same last name, he has been my life-long friend and yearly fishing buddy. One night at the campfire as we reminisced, he paused and then hit me with this profound truth. For every musician, it rings true. Stay on it, stay true, and you will eventually get your long-awaited "yes" response.)

www.GatewayEntertainment.com

RYMAN AUDITORIUM IN NASHVILLE, TENNESSEE
2010